# KARAMBIT

# KARAMBIT

## EXOTIC WEAPON OF THE INDONESIAN ARCHIPELAGO

### STEVE TARANI

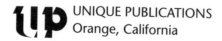
UNIQUE PUBLICATIONS
Orange, California

**Disclaimer**

Please note that the author and publisher of this book are NOT RESPON-SIBLE in any manner whatsoever for any injury that may result from practicing the techniques and/or following the instructions given within. Since the physical activities described herein may be too strenuous in nature for some readers to engage in safely, it is essential that a physician be consulted prior to training.

**Warning**

Always train with training weapons only! Under no circumstances should training with real edged weapons be attempted.

First published in 2002 by Unique Publications.

Library of Congress Catalog Number: 2002012711
ISBN: 0-86568-206-2

Unique Publications
265 S. Anita Dr. Ste. 120
Orange, CA 92868
(800) 332–3330
Second edition
05 04 03 02 01 00 99 98 97 1 3 5 7 9 10 8 6 4 2

Printed in the United States of America

Editor: John S. Soet
Design: Patrick Gross
Cover Design: George Chen

# DEDICATION

*This book is dedicated with honor and
loving respect to the memory of my master
Guru Besar Herman Suwanda—
Terimah kahsi Bapak.*

# Foreword

The study of Pencak Silat and the Karambit, much like the study of any other martial art should be considered a lifetime endeavor. To say that you can learn all there is to learn about a particular subject from any one book or any one video or even any one teacher for that matter, is illusory.

The history, basic foundation and operation of the Karambit, is an all-encompassing study requiring years of devotion and physical conditioning.However, this manuscript is offered as a fundamental training guide for the beginning student of the Karambit and is by no means intended to replace the earnest instruction of a qualified teacher.

Some will argue that the techniques and principles included herein do not reflect the full breadth and scope of practical application of the Karambit with regards to its formidable potential as an offensive weapon. In response to this argument, please bear in mind that our society has unfortunately bred certain individuals who would use such power and training in an offensive and immoral manner. Thus, for this exact reason, various aspects of training and specific technologies have been purposely omitted from this manuscript so as to present operation of the Karambit as a reasonable, controlled and responsible self-defense skill only.

Via the dissemination of this ancient technology it is my most sincere intention to bring honor and respect to the known and unknown masters who have sacrificed everything including their own personal freedom and very lives to keep this dying art alive.

# ACKNOWLEDGEMENTS

Humbly, I would like to extend my most sincere gratitude to Guro Dan Inosanto, Bapak Suherman, Pak Akyat, Cikgu Sulaiman Sharif and the entire Suwanda family for without their influence and guidance this opportunity would not be made possible. Additionally I would like to personally thank Tim Lau, Romi Archer, Tim Egberts, Ben Salas and Brian Everett for their unconditional support and contributions to this project.

# Contents

# INTRODUCTION

Located 26 miles North of Prescott, Arizona on more than 1,000 acres of rugged terrain, Gunsite Academy, one of the largest and most prestigious firearms and edged weapons training facilities in the world, provides ongoing training for many of the finest firearms trainers, qualifying civilians and members of the most demanding military, law enforcement and government agencies. Among the most heavily researched and developed training programs at Gunsite Academy next to the tactical firearms training courses, are the edged weapon training courses.

As a senior defensive tactics instructor and training consultant for law enforcement training academies, federal agent training, and U.S. State Dept. officer survival training programs, I have the responsibility of training many students across the globe in the usage of fixed and folding blades in close quarter combat. A sub-section of tactical edged weapons training programs delivered as part of my responsibility includes a briefing on the usage of exotic edged weapons.

Of these exotic edged weapons, both military/ law enforcement and defense-minded civilian students alike are most fascinated by the Indonesian Karambit. The most common questions asked are about the origins and usage of this mysterious and uniquely curved blade. This manuscript, in response to such inquiries, is intended as an attempt at providing cursory exposure to the origins, modern adaptation and training method of the Karambit—personal defense of the ancient warriors of West Java.

Licensed to teach in the Indonesian Mande Mude Pencak Silat system in July of 1996, and having been trained in the traditional usage of the Karambit both in Indonesia and the U.S. under a number of different masters, I was most fortunate to have been granted the opportunity to study with my primary teacher, the head of Pencak Silat Mande Muda International, Guru Besar Herman Suwanda, specifically in the development, operation and practical application of the Karambit.

*Guru Besar Suwanda in classic Pencak Silat fighting postures.*
*(Part of Karambit Juru.)*

*Author learning ancient Karambit*
*fighting postures from Bapak Suherman*
*in a village in West Java.*

Through the years of intense study, Pendekar Suwanda shared with me not only the mechanics of operation and training drills but also the rich and colorful history of how and why the Karambit, one of the most respected and ancient blades of Indonesia, came to be in its current form.

Throughout the remainder of this book I have made every attempt at staying as close to the traditional Indonesian training methods and oral history as it was passed on to me by my masters.

## What Exactly is a Karambit?

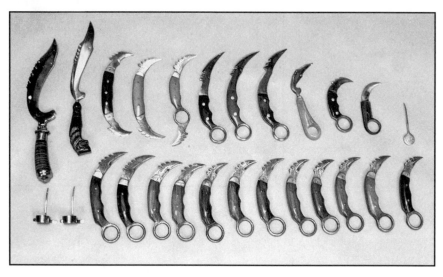

*Author's private collection of Karambits from the Philippines,
Malaysia and Indonesia. Note different sizes, shapes, and styles.*

The first question that comes to mind is "What exactly is a Karambit?" The Karambit can be defined as a small hand-held, curved fixed blade carried for personal-defense. Similar to the relationship of the Pugio (Roman Dagger) to the Gladius (Sword of the ancient Roman Legions), the Daga to the Espada (Spain), the Wakazashi to the Katana (Japan) or the Dirk to the Basket-hilt (Scotland), the Main Gauche to Le Sabre (France) and the Dagger to the Rapier (England) the Karambit is considered a "backup" or "partner" weapon and a secondary line of defense.

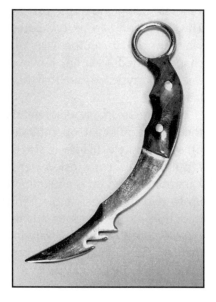

*Long Stem Steel Karambit (Sundanese)*

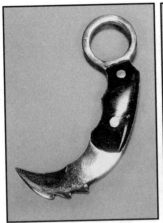

Short Stem Steel Karambit
(Filipino)

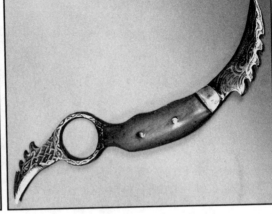

Rajawali (bird's head) style Karambit
(Malaysian)

As a side note for those serious students of ethnology, the word "Karambit" is sometimes confused with the same word from one of the 826 languages of Papua New Guinea known as "Kapriman" which is spoken near Bahinemo in the East Sepik Province along the Korosameri River. This confusion can be compared to that of the Filipino word "Barong" which in certain southern languages refers to a type of hand-held, leaf-shaped edged weapon, however, the exact same word (and spelling) refers to a type of shirt that is worn in public in more central/northern languages.

There are many different styles and shapes of Karambits, however, the most significant operational difference between the Karambit and other hand-held blades is strike delivery. A conventional straight edge requires one arm motion per one strike in only one direction. The Karambit, however, as a function of the forefinger and thumb grip, allows up to two strikes per single arm motion in either a vertical *or* horizontal direction—a tremendous advantage—especially at close and extreme close quarters range. It is very important to note that this ancient implement has traditionally been used only for self-defense and should continue to only be used as such.

## History of the Karambit

Blade designs of Indonesia were heavily influenced by the migrating Hindus of the early 6th century AD.For example, the curves of the Kris took the shape of fire. This was very symbolic to the early Hindus since fire was a symbol of life and death—quoted from the ancient Vedic prose "from ashes to ashes." In those days a Kris was created by a sword-smith to exactly match the spirit of the fighter for which it was designed. If the fighter was aggressive then the temperance of the blade was made to be aggressive. If the fighter was passive (or a counter fighter) then the temperance of the blade was made passive. It was all based upon the "prana" or life/spiritual energy of the combatant by which the smithy would design his Kris.

Thus, the warriors of that age claimed that the Kris had a certain power. This is why many old tales of the blade spoke of a "magic" of the Kris whereas it seemed to move magically in one fighter's hand but when wielded by another of equal skill, it seemed like dead weight.

Centuries ago, prior to AD1289, most of West Java was part of theindigenous Pajajaran kingdom. The Badui tribe of West Java, the aboriginal people of Sunda, considered to be the ethnic group of the Pajajaran, lived relatively peacefully until the coming of theMajapahit empire in AD1351. At that time the Badui tribe quickly migrated to the mountainous regions, brought their weapons with them and remained self-governed. Thus, the word *Badui* literally translates to "the people who won't follow the rules."

The kings of the ancient Sundanese kingdom were considered very powerful. When a king died, it was believed, by his subjects, that his spirit went into the jungles and became the spirit of the tiger. There are two terms for the tiger. One is Harimau which is the generic Bahasay Indonesian word for tiger and the other is Pak Macan (pronounced "Pah-mah-chahn. Sometimes anglicized and spelled Pamacan) which loosely translates to "great tiger." It is this exact reason the great tiger is very much revered by the Sundanese.

So awed were the ancient Sunda peoples by the power and ferocity of the Pamacan, that the common blade of the people was patterned after the shape of the claw of Pamacan. This blade was known as Kuku Macan or "claw of Pamacan." Literally translated as "tiger claw" the Kuku Macan was revered symbolically as well as practically employed.

Originally wielded in battle, the oversized Kuku Macan was a bit cumbersome to manipulate so it was scaled down to smaller sizes which augmented maneuverability. Various permutations of the Kuku Macan were developed based upon practical usage. As the saying goes "necessity is the mother of invention," the blade design came in smaller sizes and eventually found itself in the smallest size—the very personalized Karambit.

*Map of the Indonesian Archipelago*

The Karambit can be traced from Sumatra to Malaysia and Java. The Karambit of Lombok, (the island found near Bali and East Java—more specifically the island of Sumbawa), is traditionally a larger or "battlefield sized" karambit and is much larger than its more personal-sized Javanese cousin. There is also another variation of the Karambit which comes from Madura Island located northeast of Java) which is more curved known as the Clurit. There are also many different shapes and designs of the Karambit such as Rajawali (bird head shape) and others which include protruding spurs used for *tearing* flesh in the heat of battle.

The Karambit is also referred to as the Kuku Bima (literally "the claw of Bima"). Pre-12th century influence as a result of Hindus settling in Indonesian archipelago, brought the *Mahabharata* ("great epic of the Bharata Dynasty") and the *Ramayana*, (two major epics of India, valued for both high literary merit and religious inspiration), to Java. Contained within the *Mahabharata* is the *Bagavadgita* ("the Lord's song") which is the single most important religious text of Hinduism. Bima is a character from the Mahabrapta.

Also known as Kuku Hanuman (literally "the claw of Hanuman"—a character from the Ramayana), the Karambit, magical claw which protrudes from between the center of the hands of Bima and Hanuman, has become the weapon of the traditional arts of the Indonesian archipelago namely Pencak Silat.

*Hanuman,*
*Warrior Prince of the Ramayana*

The combination of the original design of the tiger's claw combined with the hand weapons of the ancient characters of the *Mahabharata* and the *Ramayana*—the Kuku Macan, Kuku Bima or Kuku Hanuman has evolved into what is known in modern times as the Karambit. It is now recognized internationally as a traditional weapon of Indonesian Pencak Silat.

Normally, in ancient times, when a fighter unsheathed a battlefield Karambit, the cutting edge was almost always smeared with some type of deadly poison which acted almost instantly upon entry into the bloodstream via laceration of the flesh. Even the smallest cut was good enough to get the poison into the bloodstream. Knowledge and usage of poisons derived from various species of poisonous frogs, snakes, scorpions and spiders were considered an essentialelement of a warrior's arsenal of close quarter combative skills. These poisons rapidly accelerated death and were most feared for their nearly instantaneous killing power. This is another reason why Pencak Silat techniques and systems such as Sabetan and Rhikasan focus on the immobilization of the hands at close quarters.

The personal Karambit (smaller version of the battlefield Karambit) was primarily designed for targeting the nerves and joints. As a result of such a small cutting surface, most cuts cannot be made deep enough to kill someone. That is why the karambit is considered a personal self-defense weapon. In contrast, the blade of the Karambit Besar (larger or battlefield version of the personal-sized Karambit) is longer and thus permits deeper cuts. According to the ancients, the battlefield Karambit was preferred not only for it's superior length but for the fact that you could, as a result of the lengthy cutting edge, "spill the entrails of your enemies onto the ground."

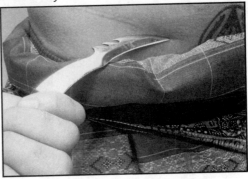

The personal Karambit targets include : Eyes, testicles, the Achilles tendon, carotid artery, biceps, forearm and wrist. A particularly nasty target of ancient times was the clavicle (collar-bone). Executed perfectly the Karambit would catch the collarbone (tip pointed down) and is then quickly turned from palm down position to palm up position which, using your body weight, would snap the bone thus rendering your enemy's weapon arm useless.

*The Karambit was specifically designed for usage in battle at close quarters.*

Specifically designed as a close quarter self-defense weapon, the Karambit is additionally quite difficult to see in the hand due to its method of deployment and cover of the fingers. Doubly menacing is that it cannot be disarmed as a result of its forefinger grip design. It is unique to any other blade as it can be used for both a medium and close fighting ranges without changing distance of the striking arm. It is also the only blade that can cut twice with a single arm stroke. All other blades need one motion for one cut. The Karambit is unique because:

It cannot be easily seen.

It cannot be easily disarmed

It can change ranges without body movement

It can deliver two cuts in a single motion.

Although quite a remarkable weapon, and as fierce as it looks, it's primary application is self defense. Its small tip and blade length are not conducive to delivery of lethal blows and the Karambit cannot be used for deep penetration thrusting and thus cannot be considered a dagger. However, when used correctly it can deliver a nasty and menacing payload to any threatening extended limb.

Originally used for personal backup, there were specific styles and systems of training which employed the Karambit as an "add on." For example, the Cikalong and Rhikasan systems of Mande Muda Pencak Silat, are the base systems of hand immobilization and close quarter technique. Once you became proficient in these systems in empty hand application, you could then easily "add on" the Karambit to your technique. This would be like attaching nuclear warheads to your conventional missiles.

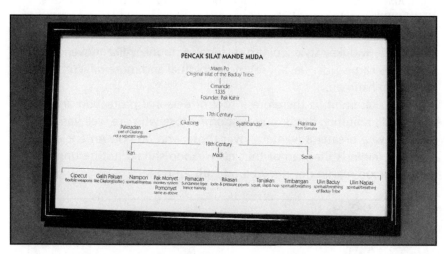

*Mande Muday Family System Tree*

Brief description of the original 18 styles which make up the Mande Muda Pencak Silat System:

HARIMAU—The tiger (from Sumatra)

MADI—Name of a respected instructor noted for his "jumping style"

RHIKESAN—Breaking, joint locks, pressure points, sensitivity.

CIPECUT—Whip, Sarung, flexible weapons application.

SERAK—Name of a respected instructor noted for his exceptional use of only 6 Jurus

CIMANDE—Name of a village noted for its superior usage of the forearms and strong stances due to leg strength developed by standing in the Cimande River.

CIKALONG—Name of a village who's practitioners favor hard style take-downs and throws from outside entries.

SYABANDAR—Name of a respected instructor who favored hard style take-downs and throws from inside entries.

KARI—Name of a respected instructor who favored the use of "Scissor hands."

TIMBANGAN—Breathing and meditation with movement

NAMPON—Name of a respected instructor who taught a noted system of breathing and meditation without physical movement.

TANJAKAN—Hill style—very hard style.

ULIN NAPAS—To use breathing or breath.

PALARADAN—Kembangan—flowery dance to develop fluid movement.

ULIN BUDUY—Technique derived from the Buduy people of ancient Sunda.

GALIH PAKHAN—A system akin to the Cikalong village style.

PAMONYET—Monkey style (spirit or essence of monkey-like movement)

PAMACAN—Large Tiger (Javanese) more spiritual and more difficult to teach than harimau.

The Karambit, is therefore a tool of personal protection and represents, skill, maturity, honor and wisdom. Those who are well versed in its usage have a greater advantage over those who do not. An ancient code of ethics reminds the warrior that his weapon should not be unsheathed without good reason nor draw blood without honor.

*Guru Besar Suwanda, Steve Tarani and Bapak Suherman in Indonesia.*

# PART ONE

---

# BASIC HANDLING
# AND
# OPERATION

---

## *Indonesian Training Terminology*

Before we get started in our training, most of the terminology found in this manuscript is in plain English. However, adhering to austere training traditions, there are certain words and phrases employed by my masters, which are maintained for integrity. My primary instructor, Guru Besar Pendekar Herman Suwanda spoke many dialects and completely different languages such as Bahasay Indonesian (the national language of Indonesia) Sudanese, the native language of various tribes originating in West Java and a number of others. Thus, the exact translation of the terms below may vary depending upon to which village you travel.

KIRI—The left or to the left hand side

KANAN—The right or to the right hand side

JURU—A singular technique or movement without a partner. Similar to shadow boxing (Western Boxing), Dtoi Lom (Thai Boxing) or Kata (Karate)

KAKACANGAN—A multiple of Jurus (more than one juru)

BUAH—Executed technique or movement with a training partner.

GUNTING—Scissors-like motion. This is the exact same word in Tagalog (national language of the Philipppines). Certain words in Tagalog such as Gunting, Bulan, Lima and others are identical to those of Bahasay Indonesian.

KUDA KUDA—Horse stance or horse-like posture. This can either be with legs wide, as in the example of sitting on the back of a horse, or legs narrow as in the placement of the horses hooves when walking.

HARIMAU—Tiger or tiger style

ANAK HARIMAU—Literally "son of the Tiger" usually referring to either a sub-system or a definite posture (usually kneeling and/ or lower to the ground)

*Harimau Stance—low kneeling.*

DUDUK—Seated or sitting stance or posture.

TANGAN—Hand or having to do with the hands.

KOBOK—Takedown, throw or trip using the arms.

KAHKI—Legs or having to do with the legs.

LEDOK—Takedown, throw or trip using the legs.

GOLANG—Circle or circular movement usually in a wide circumference

TOTOK—Use of pressure points in reference to placement of blade tip

PICAHAN—Literally "broken apart" such as glass or shattered coffee cup. A term applied to practical application of technique where a student (after achieving a deep understanding of basic movements and standard technique) has learned to "use the pieces" to create any solution on the fly as needed in the heat of actual combat.

MASUK—"The way in," entry, pathway or entrance. Usually used in the context of the opening move in a technique.

TUHOD—knee or of relating to manipulation of the knees.

*Anak Harimau Stance—
kneeling lower to the earth.*

## Parts of the Karambit

There are several identifiable parts of any Karambit. Much like there are many different cars, there are many different Karambits. Every car must have a set of tires, an engine of some kind and some type of body in order for it to be a car. The same thing applies to a Karambit. There are unlimited styles and shapes of Karambits, however there are certain basic parts. These are illustrated below:

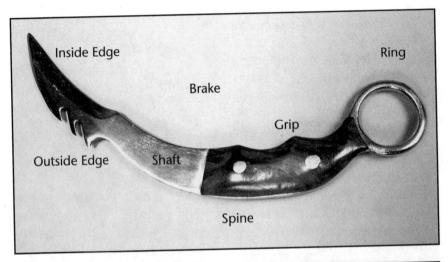

There are also what is known as the "dominant edge." This is where there may be a design with a single bevel. According to the masters there is less friction when the number of bevels is equal to one during a cut or puncture. The dominant edge for a right handed practitioner would be on the inside (bevel to the left) with the flat on the outside. The dominant edge for a left-handed practitioner would also be on the inside (bevel to the right) with the flat on the outside. One of the keys to selecting a "dominant edge" style Karambit is to remember that the flat is always to the outside.

When first learning how to manipulate the Karambit it is highly suggested that you begin with a trainer model. My highest recommendation would either be the Sharkee Karambit (high impact plastic) or the Edges2 Training Karambit (aluminum). Both of these manufacturers are long time students of the edged weapon and take great pride in their work. These training Karambits have

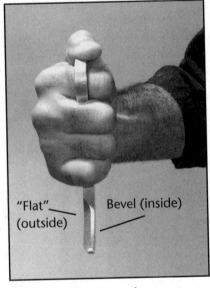

*Dominant edge.*

my 100% percent endorsement of quality trainers—exactly perfect for the application of this material.

As there are a multitude of live or actual Karambits so are there a multitude of types of trainers. The advantages of wood are that they are easy and inexpensive to make. However these are the easiest to break and splinter during training. Next up would be high-impact resin or plastic. These are light,

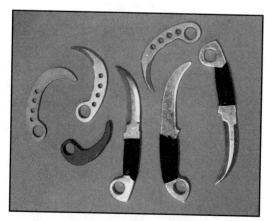

*Variety of aluminum and plastic training Karambits.*

inexpensive, durable and quite forgiving on your own body as well as that of your training partner. Aluminum, on the other hand, is quite unforgiving, however it offers the closest feel and operational characteristics of the real thing.

Again, for those interested in seriously training, I cannot recommend any higher quality training Karambits than those produced by Sharkee Inc (high impact plastic) and Edges2 (aluminum)—each can be found on the interenet. Another great source for training products is www.karambit.com.

The choice of which training karambit to buy is trulty a subjective decision. However, for your own safety and for the safety of those around you it is imperative when training to ALWAYS USE YOUR TRAINING KARAMBIT.

## Gripping the Karambit

There are several ways to hold the Karambit. General usage calls for the classical grip of index finger through the ring and the remaining fingers around the grip with baby finger lightly perched just above the very bottom edge.

There are two types of common grip. One is retracted and the other is extended.

The Retracted position calls for a solid index finger position well past the second knuckle of the index finger. The remaining grip should be firm around the grip. The thumb can either be placed directly on the ring or on your fingers. Each position has its advantages and disadvantages and ultimately remains a matter of operator discretion.

*Retracted with "thumb on."*

*Retracted with "thumb off."*

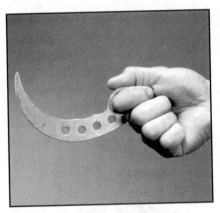

*Extended with "thumb on."*

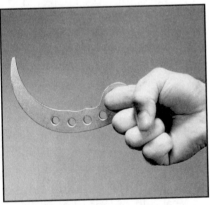

*Extended with "thumb off."*

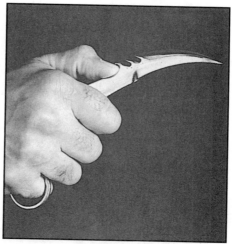

*Alternate finger grips used for other types of Karambits.*

Regardless of what type of grip you select, the fingers should be firmly gripping to ensure good control and solid points of contact throughout the entire available surface of the grip and ring.

## Operational Hand Postures

There are three basic hand positions that must be clearly understood before moving on. These are Palm up, Palm Down and Palm Vertical postures.

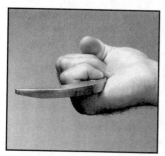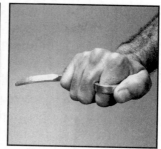

*Palm up.*

*Palm down with "thumb off."*

*Palm down with "thumb on."*

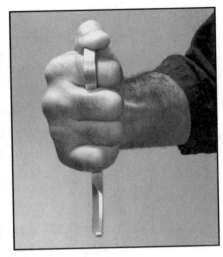

*Palm vertical.*

## Operational Body Postures

Standing, kneeling and sitting postures, unique to the art of Pencak Silat when handling the Karambit, is the changing of elevation during any engagement. In order to achieve proficiency at these different elevations we must practice manipulation and movement of each level.

The blade is generally positioned at your centerline approximately at your chin level always with the safety hand behind it for backup.

### STANDING (KUDA KUDA):

The human body uses symmetry for its balance during mobility. Thus when we walk, the mechanics of human ambulation dictate that an opposing foot must move forward simultaneously with an opposing hand. In other words, if you step forward with your right foot, then your left hand naturally moves forward when you walk. Unlike the robot-like motion of right foot moving forward with right hand and the left foot moving forward with the left hand, the human body depends heavily upon balance and symmetry for its mobility.

In the standing position—start with hands by your side and start walking normally forward. Now freeze in this natural position and crouch down like a tiger. Proper body position is with the blade is back by the

*Natural Forward mobility
(walking).*

*Kuda Kuda
(forward standing horse stance).*

body and the lead hand is out in front and then switch positions of the hand and blade as you move forward.

This technology is very similar to that of the Filipino method of never extending both the knife and safety hand at the same time. It's always either one or the other that is forward in motion.

## KNEELING (HARIMAU):

The Japanese *seiza* (two-point seated posture) method of knee walking as taught in Aikido or classical Japanese Jiu-Jitsu is quite similar to the Indonesian method in that movement is linear with respect to forward body position.

The Indonesian method forms a solid three-point stance with weight evenly distributed and can be advantageously shifted either forward or backward based on desired direction of movement. Unlike the linear movement of the Japanese method, Harimau knee walking movements are predominantly angular or *golang* style (circular) to emulate the movements of Pak Macan in pre-engagement posture.

*Traditional Japanese
seiza position.*

*Traditional Harimau*
*(three-point stance).*

Much akin to standing, the human body uses symmetry for its balance during mobility and thus hand posture for kneeling should exactly match that of standing. Similar to standing (Kuda Kuda), Karambit handling in kneeling (Harimau) is very similar to that of the Filipino method of never extending both the knife and safety hand at the same time.

## SITTING (DUDUK):

The concept of "walking" in seated position may seem somewhat foreign to Westerners. However sitting and seated walking in this manner is quite popular in countries such as India, Malaysia and Indonesia, thus important to be able to defend yourself from this position as well as kneeling and standing.

*Traditional Duduk Posture.*

We as humans can ambulate even from a seated posture and must also be able to defend ourselves when walking seated.

## Training Method

The training method of the Karambit is broken down into two simple divisions: the mental and the physical. As with most martial sciences, Pencak Silat requires that basic movements be executed in the air without a partner or any training equipment. The movements (similar to shadow boxing) are called *Jurus*. Thus when studying a base system such as Cikalong, Cimande or Syabandar, it is important to become fluid in your movement and execution. Applying these same techniques with a training partner are known as *Buah*. Not used so much with jurus but used more with technique, the Karambit must move comfortably and fluidly in your hand in harmony with the basic movements of the specific empty-hand system.

*Author training with Guru Besar Suwanda in West Java.*

Skill and proficiency with the Karambit derives originally from the empty hand and is broken down into what is known as positive energy and negative energy. If you initiate a strike, this is considered "positive energy." If you are reacting to a strike, this is considered "negative energy." These are considered positive and negative techniques when deploying the Karambit in self-defense.

The Sundanese philosophy of Agama Kuring (indigenous religious philosophy of the Sunda people) expounds a combination of mental, physical and spiritual aspects to both empty hand and edged weapon combat. There exists a degree of confidence or certainty which arises from "knowing" that you can cut. There is an old saying that "strong intention is strong foundation." Very similar to Bruce Lee's explanation in the Tao of Jeet Kune Do that if a man is really focused on biting your nose and it is his most powerful intention to do so, then there's just about nothing you can do to stop him.

Thus, in training with the Karambit, you must begin with a strong foundation. A strong foundation is nothing more than focused intention. There must then be a mental correlation between "goal" and "result." For example, if immobilizing your attacker is considered the *result* of defending against an attack, then you have reached your *goal* of walking away unharmed. This is simply a matter of mental application to familiarized technique. This is purely a spiritual/ mental conceptualization. No martial arts training is needed for projection of intention and visualization as this is a function of *mental* conditioning. According to Agama Kuring—your belief causes your reality.

The ancients had a method of training (which can be found in very few villages in modern days) known as "marrying the Kambangan." The Kambangan is a series of Jurus that is executed to music. Hundreds and sometimes thousands of repetitions (based on calculations involving your birth date and day) are executed in a ceremonial and serious manner with *intention*. As a result of such rigorous engraining of muscle memory with focused intention, your mentality becomes "married" to your mechanical or physical movement—the two become one.

## Combat Strategy

Mental training also includes strategy. Much like a chess match, you must be simultaneously aware of your attacker's possible moves as much as you are focused on your own. Predominantly a reactive or "counter" method of deployment, execution of defensive strike patterns is a matter of timing and placement.

One of the most important strategic maneuvers is the "condition of neutrality." This can be compared to driving a truck with a stick shift. When you are in first gear and you need to get into second or possibly third, because you're going rapidly down a hill, you must first press in the clutch to get to neutral and then put it into the gear you want. When you stop the vehicle you shift into neutral and then put it in gear when the timing is right to catch the green light.

Conceptually, you don't ever want to be "stuck in any one gear," you want to always have your clutch depressed or in neutral ready to engage the proper gear with the appropriate timing.

The Indonesian masters have a term for this called "letting him into your house." The idea is to "let him into your house" and then let *him* tell you where he wants to go—this will allow you simple decisions based on his movements. How do you know when to change elevation or whether to change ranges or to hit high or to hit low targets? You let him "tell" you by his movement.

*Unassuming MASUK (entry)*
*"letting him into your*
*house" posture.*

Best is to begin in a neutral position. You should start in the middle (focus the edge and tip at the cross hairs of his belt line and center mass) and then after his opening you can go high or low. Changing elevations with footwork and simultaneously changing ranges with the weapon give you the tactical advantage when playing the counter-offensive strategy.

Equally as important as neutrality is gauging distance. There are two factors that come into play when gauging distance. One is speed and the other is power.

If you need to quickly deliver a heavy payload across a great distance you need a lot of power. For example, a vehicle hauling 40 tons of cargo from Los Angeles to New York needs a really powerful engine to deliver its contents. For more distance you need more power. Conversely, if you have two orange parking cones set up only a quarter-mile apart and you want to get from one to the other as quickly as possible, then you need a small, light vehicle that can travel very fast. For short distances you need more speed.

The same concept applies to fighting. If you're trying to reach this guy's face from five or six feet away, then you need to generate quite a bit of power to close such a long distance. If your blade starts out only a few inches from his wrist then it's just a matter of increasing your speed.

## Training Summary

To successfully defend yourself from any incoming strike using the Karambit, like any other weapon of the martial arts, you need at least basic training. Proficiency with the Karambit is broken down into three major divisions:

1. FOUNDATION—Mental or spiritual (intention/ visualization)
2. STRATEGY—(neutrality—letting him into your house: more distance = more power; less distance = more speed)
3. TECHNIQUE—physical movement

We, as Westerners must keep in mind that these combat technologies come from what is called a "blade culture."

In the far East, such a blade culture welcomes a boy to manhood when he is given his first blade. It is a symbol of maturity and responsibility. This can be somewhat comparable to dad giving you the keys to the car for the very first time, but it still doesn't capture the same significance and essence of true rite of passage as does the blade cultures.

According to the tradition of blade cultures, the man and blade are always together. They are considered a single unit. A man without his blade is comparable to man without his penis.

The karambit, is therefore a tool of personal protection and represents, skill, maturity, honor and wisdom. Those who are well versed in its usage have a greater advantage over those who do not. An ancient code of ethics reminds the warrior that his weapon should not be unsheathed without good reason nor draw blood without honor.

## Leg Training Drill #1

One of my first Malaysian teachers Cikgu Sulaimen Sharif, Imam Khalifah of the Silat Seni Gayong system in America, once shared with me: "Steve, the car cannot go anywhere without the tires." What he meant by this was that without strong legs, your ability to move swiftly and with purpose is compromised.

*Author and Cikgu Sulaimen Sharif, (Imam Khalifah Gayong Amerika) circa 1989.*

Whenever training in Indonesia, I witness the movement and power of the masters with such grace and prowess as to rival that of the big cats. When I asked them how I could develop such strength, grace and speed of movement, they replied— "You do like this..."

One of the best training drills to develop this ability to change elevations is to start from the standing horse stance (KUDA KUDA), drop one leg down into kneeling (HARIMAU), drop to DUDUK and then lightly bounce both feet off the ground back to KUDA KUDA posture. Practice this both left and right side. At first your legs will tire out relatively quickly (maybe only ten or twelve reps). Eventually you will be able to last for up to 20 or 30 minutes. The end result is that your leg strength is tremendously increased and with it comes speed and power in movement.

*Traditional standing (Kuda Kuda) posture.*

*Drop one leg down into Harimau kneeling posture.*

*Your tail and both legs should be touching the earth.*

*Now rock forward.*

*Traditional Duduk posture facing the opposite way.*

## *Extension and Retraction*

As mentioned earlier the main difference between this curved blade and the typical Occidental straight edge is that there exists the option for two cuts for every one arm movement. Let's take a closer look at these operating principles.

There are only two blade positions in the operation of the Karambit:

*The Karambit in retracted position.*

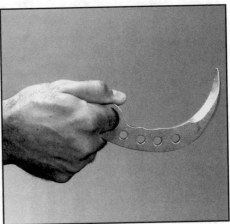

*The Karambit in extended position.*

RETRACTION/EXTENSION
TRAINING DRILL #1
(VERTICAL)

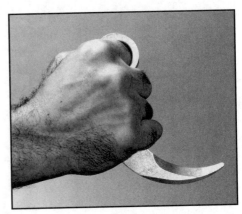

*Start with Karambit
in retracted position.*

*Open fingers and push away from your body.*

*The Karambit in extended position.*

*Open fingers and pull back toward your body.*

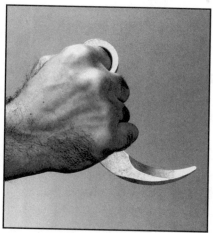

*End with Karambit in retracted position.*

Remember to always return to proper defensive posture with the hands.

RETRACTION/ EXTENSION
TRAINING DRILL #2
(HORIZONTAL)

*Start with Karambit in
retracted position.*

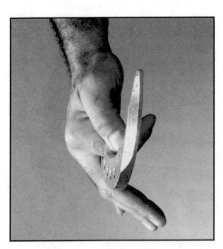

*Open fingers and push away
from your body.*

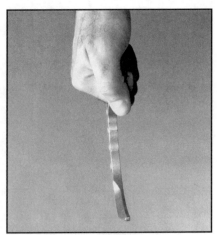

*The Karambit in
extended position.*

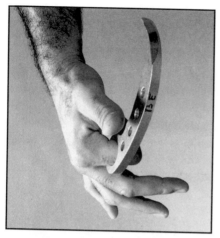

*Open fingers and pull back
toward your body.*

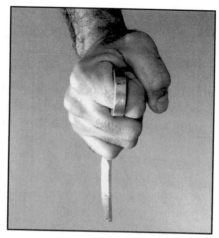

*End with Karambit in
retracted position.*

## Progression of Training

The master says: "Those who chose to carry [the Karambit] also chose the responsibility to train [with it]." No truer words have been spoken about this most interesting and exotic blade.

To operate proficiently means to train proficiently. You've heard the old adage "perfect practice makes perfect." This is especially true in the case of training with the Karambit. Unlike most traditional blade systems, the Karambit requires development of the human body, the human mind and that aspect of our humanity which is beyond the body and the mind. Training with the body is only one third of the equation—the rest comes later.

If you were fighting elbow to elbow in the ancient Roman Legions marching with your sword drawn and shield raised running head first into the fray of battle, you would have nothing but your equipment and your training to depend upon for your survival. The same if you were a part of an elite commando unit or special operations team. It boils down to the two most important aspects of weapons systems—your hardware and your training.

Thus, in the case of the Karambit, training is of utmost importance. You wouldn't go out there on the freeway with a big-rig if you had never driven an eighteen-wheel truck before. As a matter of fact you'd probably want to get some training in a parking lot or driveway long before you ended up on a crowded freeway traveling at speeds near 75 miles per hour. You never want to operate outside your capacity for proficiency. The Karambit is the same way. If you don't know how to properly handle and operate your Karambit, you could end up hurting yourself or even those around you.

One humid and rainy equatorial afternoon, sitting in a training camp located in a valley nestled between two volcanoes in West Java, Guru Besar Suwanda spoke at great length on the progression of training to a small group of American Pencak Silat Instructors of which I was quite fortunate to be included.

*Rare shot of Guru Besar Suwanda lecturing to us with one of his original teachers Pak Odid in Jawa Barat, Indonesia.*

It was a magnificent lecture. Although he provided enough info to fill several volumes, due to space constraints for this book, it was necessary to break down the data he shared with us into an outline form. The lecture, a summary in itself, was distilled from a MASSIVE body of historical knowledge passed down from master to student by word of mouth since before the 12th century AD:

Juru—The student must first come to fully understand the movement and abilities of his own body in a precise and structured format.

Buah—The student must then come to fully understand the movement and abilities of his own body in a precise and structured format in harmony with a training partner.

Karambit (and other weapons)—The student must then come to fully understand the movement and abilities of his own body in a precise and structured format in harmony with a training partner while operating hand-held extensions of his ability.

Picahan—The student must be able to employ his skills and knowledge outside of the form and rigid structure of the patterns in which he has engrained his movement—fragmented and perhaps as part of other fragments of skills to form a solution to any problem with which he may be confronted. This concept transcends the physical and mental application.

Actual Combat—Only after achieving success via application of Picahan can a student self-develop the capability and degree of competence and confidence necessary to pull it all off in the live fire of actual combat.

The brevity and conciseness of the above summary truly does not do justice to the tremendous breadth and scope of what Pak Herman covered in that lecture. However, for purposes of this manuscript it needed be limited in context.

## SAFETY

The primary consideration of training is always safety. This must be placed first and foremost in the list of priorities. As suggested earlier, it is my recommendation to find yourself a quality karambit trainer and put your real one in the drawer until you feel like you can "drive on the freeway" so to speak.

One of the best sets of training equipment out there for usage when training with the Karambit is LAMECO training gear. This unique training equipment was developed by Punong Guro Edgar G. Sulite for the purposes of protecting the hands and arms when training for edged weapons. This way one can train safely yet realistically without incurring the risks that unprotected body parts may possibly sustain.

*The LAMECO Wrist Guard.*

*The LAMECO Hand Guard.*

## *Standard Operation*

There are three basic types of operation with the Karambit:
- Hacking
- Slashing
- Thrusting

There are others such as scraping and coring which we may address in later training manuscripts. However, for purposes of this level of training we will focus on the primary types of operation.

*Practical self-defense application with the Karambit.*

Standard operation can be executed from either of two positions of operation:
- Hacking, slashing or thrusting from retracted position
- Hacking, slashing or thrusting from extended position

Hacking is the act of striking downward and bouncing back as in the motion of chopping carrots. Hacking is generally executed with only the outside edge of the Karambit.

*Hacking with the Karambit in self-defense.*

Slashing is the act of drawing across an area from one side to the other while maintaining consistent contact of the blade to the cutting surface. Slashing is mostly executed by the outside edge with some exceptions which allow contact with the inside edge.

Thrusting is simply a matter of punching the tip or point forward, up or down in such a manner as to puncture a specific target area.

*Self defense using a hooking technique with the Karambit.*

## Starting and Ending Operational Postures

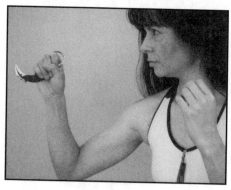 

*Practical operational postures.*

There are seven starting and ending operational postures with the Karambit:

- High Center Posture
- High Open Side Posture
- High Closed Side Posture
- Low Center Posture
- Low Open Side Posture
- Low Closed Side Posture
- Standard Ready Posture

*High Center Posture.*

*Low Center Posture.*

*High Open Side Posture.*

*Low Open Side Posture.*

*High Closed Side Posture.*

*Low Closed Side Posture.*

*Standard Ready Posture.*

## Ranges and Positions of Engagement

Long range—neither can reach the other (from either retracted or extended)

Close range—both can touch the other and(from either retracted or extended)

Before we start any training drills with our training partner it's necessary to gauge for proper training distance pertinent to which drill we are training

*Long Range Extended.*

*Close Range Extended.*

*Long Range Retracted.*

*Close Range Retracted.*

Before we get into the actual training drills, it is important to understand the advantages and disadvantages of body position in relation to engagement with the Karambit at close quarters.

The INSIDE position is where you find yourself in that area facing your opponent where you end up between both of his arms.

*Inside position.*

The disadvantage of this position is that he has access to you at close range with both his knife, opposite hand, elbows, knees, both feet and possibly a head butt.

The ON-LINE position is where you find yourself in that area facing your opponent where you end up aligned directly in front of his attacking weapon including his striking hands and /or striking feet.

The disadvantage of this position is that he has immediate access to you at close range with his knife or forward aggressive movement. The advantage is

*On Line position.*

that you are not exposed to as potential a threat from his opposite hand, elbows, knees, both feet and possibly a head butt.

The OUTSIDE position is where you find yourself in that area facing your opponent where you end up directly on the outside of his attacking weapon including his striking hands and /or striking feet..

The advantage of this position is that he has no immediate access to you at close range with his knife or forward aggressive movement. Additionally you are not exposed to as potential a threat from his opposite hand, elbows, knees, both feet and possibly a head butt. There are no disadvantages to this position and is the best to end up if ever you find yourself in a self-defense situation.

*Outside position.*

One other distinct advantage of this position is that your moving around on the outside forces him to follow your movement. It is always the case that reaction is always slower than action. Thus you end up taking control of any situation at that point where you take control of the outside and force his reactions to your actions. This concept is quite similar to that of a boxer using ring generalmanship to control the center of the ring and thus attempt to control the fight.

An interesting observation about the outside position, especially with regards to the art of Pencak Silat, is that if you look down on both fighters from above, more than 75% of positional area belongs to the outside. The trick is to deftly maneuver from the INSIDE position past the ON-LINE position to get to all that open area on the OUTSIDE without getting caught by your opponent.

*More than 75% of positional area belongs to the outside.*

## Basic Training Drills

There are many branches of Pencak Silat. The roots of all Karambit training extend from specific systems developed in various villages throughout the Indonesian Archipelago.

For purposes of basic training we will address a specific style known as Cimande which comes from Cimande village in West Java. This particular village at which we trained, is considered the root of the Mande Muda family system of Pencak Silat. My teacher's mother (Ibu) is from this village. She and her family welcomed us on several occasions to train with the masters.

One particular trip, we arrived a little earlier than expected. As a side note, for those who have never been to a remote West Javanese village, there are no phones and no electricity. The fact that Ibu and her family were even expecting us was uncanny since there were no messengers, or any physical communication whatsoever from Lembang all the way out to Cimande (seven hours by jeep—provided no herd crossings).

Since we arrived "early," one of the senior instructors was out in the rice fields working. The villagers sent a young boy to tell the master that his (somehow) expected gusts had arrived. About a half hour later, rolling down his pant legs and rolling up his sleeves, he greeted us with a great big smile and open hands. He was a fairly small man in physical stature, perhaps 115 lbs and sleight build. However, the power in his strikes would almost knock down even the biggest heavy-weight in our group. Incredible power generated by intention and a lifetime of study and devotion to his art.

In all Karambit training it is customary to learn the movement empty hand in JURU and BUAH form. It is important to make a distinction between a JURU and a BUAH. If you remember to check the terminology chapter JURU is akin to Kata and a BUAH is when you are working with a training partner. Later on in your training you may then practice with the Karambit in both JURU and BUAH form. Remember the structure of the masters from progression of training:

- Juru
- Buah
- Karambit
- Picahan
- Actual Combat

## BASIC TRAINING DRILL #1

The empty hand JURU form of Basic Training Drill #1 is called Cimandi Juru Dalapan (or the Eighth Cimande Juru) it goes like this:

*Begin from Basic Kuda Kuda Ready Posture.*

*Move both your lead hand (palm up) and your support hand palm down to the high open operational body posture.*

The empty hand BUAH form of Basic Training Drill #1 is called Cimandi Buah Dalapan (or the Eighth Cimande Buah) it goes like this:

*Ask your training partner to deliver a slow and controlled backfist to your high line.*

*From Standard Ready Posture, receive the incoming backfist with lead hand palm up and support hand palm down.*

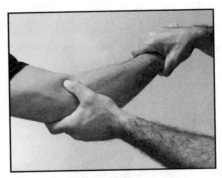

*Firmly grasp just above your partner's elbow with your lead hand and secure his wrist with your support hand pushing downward.*

Now with Karambit in hand , execute the same Juru and Buah movements. The Karambit JURU form of Basic Training Drill #1 is called Cimandi Juru Dalapan (or the Eighth Cimande Juru) it goes like this:

*Begin from Basic Kuda Kuda Ready Posture with Karambit.*

*Move both your lead hand (palm up) and your support hand palm down*
*to the high open operational body posture. Karambit should remain*
*in retraction in the PALM DOWN operational hand posture.*

In this next section we will address the Karambit Buah. Keep in mind, when practicing the Karambit Buah with your partner, be sure that he is safely equipped with quality forearm protection such as the LAMECO armguard and a training knife of your choice.

The Karambit BUAH form of Basic Training Drill #1 is called Cimandi Buah Dalapan (or the Eighth Cimande Buah) it goes like this:

*Ask your training partner to deliver*
*a slow and controlled back hand slash*
*to your high line.*

*From Standard Ready Posture, receive the incoming backhand slash with lead hand palm up and Karambit hand palm down—maintain retraction.*

*Firmly grasp just above your partner's elbow with your lead hand and secure his wrist with your Karambit.*

## BASIC TRAINING DRILL #2

The empty hand JURU form of Basic Training Drill #2 is called Cimandi Juru Satu (or the first Cimande Juru) it goes like this:

*Begin from Basic Kuda Kuda Ready Posture.*

*Move lead hand to high open and support hand to closed fist in front of your lead hand elbow.*

*Move lead hand from high outside position to your center and at the same time move your closed fist (palm down) to the outside position of your lead elbow.*

*Move support hand from in front of lead hand elbow along forearm toward your support hand high outside position and end with your lead hand palm down under and lightly touching your support hand triceps.*

*Open closed fist and turn your support hand palm down as if grasping an imaginary wrist at the same time moving your lead hand back to the center of your torso.*

*Move both your lead hand (palm up) and your support hand palm down to the center operational body posture.*

The empty hand BUAH form of Basic Training Drill #2 is called Cimandi Buah Satu (or the first Cimande Buah) it goes like this:

*Begin from basic Kuda Kuda ready posture and ask your training partner to deliver a slow and controlled straight punch to your centerline. Move lead hand to high open and support hand to closed fist in front of your lead hand elbow.*

*Move lead hand from high outside position to your center picking up the incoming delivery with vertical palm. At the same time move your closed fist (palm down) from in front of your lead elbow upward towards his extended forearm.*

*Move support hand from in front of lead hand elbow along forearm picking up your training partners extended forearm and carrying it toward your support hand high outside position and end with your lead hand palm down under and lightly touching your support hand triceps.*

*Open closed fist and turn your support hand palm down and firmly grasp your training partners wrist at the same time moving your lead hand back to just above his elbow.*

*Secure his elbow just above the elbow joint with your lead hand palm up while simultaneously applying a downward pressure on his grasped wrist with your support hand.*

Now with Karambit in hand , execute the same Juru and Buah as part of Basic Training Drill #2. When practicing the Buah with your partner, be sure that he is equipped with quality forearm protection such as the LAMECO armguard and a training knife of your choice.

The Karambit JURU form of Basic Training Drill #2 is called Cimandi Juru Satu (or the first Cimande Juru) it goes like this:

*Begin with Karambit from basic Kuda Kuda ready posture. Move lead hand to high open and Karambit hand to palm down in front of your lead hand elbow.*

*Move lead hand from high outside position to your center and at the same time move your Karambit (palm down) to the outside position of your lead elbow.*

*Move Karambit hand from in front of lead hand elbow along forearm toward your Karambit hand high outside position and end with your lead hand palm down under and nearly touching your Krambit hand triceps. Your Karambit should be in vertical palm posture.*

*Turn your Karambit hand palm down as if hooking an imaginary wrist at the same time moving your lead hand back to the center of your torso.*

*Move both your lead hand (palm up) and your Karambit hand palm down toward high center operational body posture.*

Remember safety first when training with the Karambit especially the Karambit BUAH. You should be using your training Karambit, your partner should be using his training knife and should also be wearing protective training gear such as the LAMECO wrist protector.

The Karambit BUAH form of Basic Training Drill #2 is called Cimandi Buah Satu (or the first Cimande Buah) it goes like this:

*Ask your training partner to deliver a slow and controlled straight thrust or slash to your centerline. Move lead hand to high open and Karambit hand palm down in front of your lead hand elbow.*

Move lead hand from high outside position to your center and at the same time move your Karambit hand (palm down) to the outside position of your lead elbow picking up the incoming delivery with the forearm of your Karambit hand.

Move your Karambit hand from in front of lead hand elbow along forearm picking up your training partners extended forearm and carrying it toward your Karambit hand high outside position and end with your lead hand palm down under and nearly touching your Karambit hand triceps resulting in your Karambit hand in the vertical palm posture.

Turn your Karambit hand palm down and firmly hook your training partners wrist with the Karambitat the same time moving your lead hand back to just above his elbow and apply upward pressure.

Secure his elbow just above the elbow joint with your lead hand palm up while simultaneously applying a downward pressure on his hooked wrist with your Karambit.

## BASIC TRAINING DRILL #3

The empty hand JURU form of Basic Training Drill #3 is called Syabandhar Juru Satu (or the First Syabandar Juru)it goes like this:

*Begin from Basic Kuda Kuda Ready Posture.*

*Move both your lead hand (palm up) and your support hand palm down to the high closed operational body posture.*

The empty hand BUAH form of Basic Training Drill #3 is called Syabandar Buah Satu (or the First Syabandar Buah) it goes like this:

*Ask your partner to deliver a slow and controlled wide hook to your high line. From Standard Ready Posture, receive the incoming wide hook with lead hand palm down and support hand palm up.*

*Secure his wrist with your lead hand and. firmly grasp just above your training partner's elbow with your support hand.*

*Push his attack arm down into low center position to secure superior control and balance.*

*Slide your front hand back and down to secure his wrist. Simultaneously switch your outside hand wrist grip for an outside elbow grasp.*

*Reattach your lead hand to just above his elbow joint (palm up) and maintain pressure with your support hand (palm down).*

Now with Karambit in hand, execute the same Juru and Buah as part of Basic Training Drill #3. When practicing the Buah with your partner, be sure that he is equipped with quality forearm protection such as the LAMECO armguard and a training knife of your choice.

The Karambit hand JURU form of Basic Training Drill #3 is called Syabandhar Juru Satu (or the First Syabandar Juru) it goes like this:

*Begin from Basic Kuda Kuda Ready Posture.*

*Move both your lead hand (palm up) and your Karambit hand palm down to the high closed operational body posture.*

*Turn Karambit to palm down position and lead hand to palm up position.*

*Continue pushing down with the Karambit and up with your lead hand moving toward optimum control position.*

*Move both arms toward your low center position to train yourself to always gain superior balance and control over your opponent's attacking arm.*

The Karambit BUAH form of Basic Training Drill #3 is called Syabandar Buah Satu (or the First Syabandar Buah) it goes like this:

*Ask your training partner to deliver a slow and controlled forehand slash to your high line.*

*From Standard Ready Posture, receive the incoming slash with lead hand palm down and Karambit hooking up ender the LAMECO arm guard palm up.*

In a reality situation the Karambit could be applied to the triceps just above the elbow or under the armpit at this step. On the battlefields in ancient times the hook was placed against the opponent's throat to neutralize the attack.

*Secure his wrist with your lead hand and. firmly apply pressure to the LAMECO training gear using your Karambit.*

*Now move your Karambit from the LAMECO pad on the inside to outside his extended arm while maintaining firm wrist grasp and opposing pressure to immobilize his arm.*

*Continue to move your Karambit back to your centerline carrying his arm with it and release his wrist with your lead hand.*

*Reattach your lead hand to just above his elbow joint (palm up) and hook your training partners wrist (over the training pad)and continue to apply slight pressure (palm down) so as to immobilize the arm.*

You may notice that at the end of all three of these basic training drills. You always end up in the OUTSIDE position, This is not by coincidence. Almost all the basic training drills of the original village styles end up on the OUTSIDE—safest place to be in any fight.

Remember that part about walking—position of foot and hand so far these drills have been executed from a stationary position. Later in our training we will work them into mobility drills. It's important to first master the basic movements stationary before adding rapid motion.

Now we will take our first three basic training drills and develop them into the next level of training skills.

### BASIC TRAINING DRILL #4 (BUAH TANGAN)

In this skills cluster, we will be combining the first three empty hand buahs back to back and then cycle through them in order once you've reached the last step.

*Using empty hands, face your training partner in standard ready posture (kuda kuda).*

*Training partner delivers slow and controlled backhander to the high line.*

*Execute Basic Training Drill #1 Empty Hand Buah.*

*Secure partner's attacking hand to your low center for maximum control.*

*Using empty hands, face your training partner in standard ready posture (kuda kuda).*

*Training partner delivers slow and controlled straight punch to your centerline.*

*Execute Basic Training Drill #2 Empty Hand Buah.*

*Again bring his attack arm to your low center for maximum control.*

*Using empty hands, face your training partner in standard ready posture (kuda kuda). Ask your training partner to deliver a slow and controlled wide looping hook to your high line.*

*Execute Basic Training Drill #3 Empty Hand Buah.*

*Again position yourself on the outside.*

*Bring his attacking arm to the low center position for maximum leverage and control.*

Go then back to the first step and repeat this over and over again at varying speeds.

Typical Mande Muda Training method is to first execute each of these steps in order a number of times. In other words, your training partner will deliver a backhander, then a centerline punch and then a looping wide hook, you will then execute appropriate technique and then start over from the beginning. The second stage of training is for your training partner to deliver each of the angles of attack RANDOMLY. This forces you to react appropriately with the right technique for the right delivery. After many repetitions this will become second nature to you—that's when it's time to move on to Basic Training Drill #5.

Another important training tip is as described by Guro Dan Inosanto—"When you first start to drive around a new city where you've never been, you don't really know where you're going. However, the next day you try going down this street and the next day you try going down that street and a friend says "hey try this way—it's a shortcut," and the next day you feel even more comfortable and don't even have to look at the street signs." As the days add up it becomes easier and easier to find you way around the new town. The moral of that story is that these techniques take time. However, with a sufficient number of repetitions they eventually become second nature.

There is no secret to the martial arts—the only secret if any is in the number of repetitions and the number of hours that you're willing to train.

*Author, Guru Dan Inosanto, Terry Gibson,*
*Guru Besar Suwanda and the infamous,*
*elusive Paul "Ted" Grybow.*

## BASIC TRAINING DRILL #5
## (BUAH KARAMBIT)

Now with Karambit in hand, execute the same Buahs as part of Basic Training Drill #4. When practicing the Buah with your partner, be sure that he is equipped with quality forearm protection such as the LAMECO armguard and a training knife of your choice.

*Training partner delivers slow and controlled backhand slash to the high line.*

*Execute Basic Training Drill #1 Karambit Buah.*

*Take attacking arm to optimum control position.*

*Training partner delivers slow and controlled straight line thrust to your centerline.*

*Execute Basic Training Drill #2 Karambit Buah.*

*Again control attacking arm to optimum position.*

*Using empty hands, face your training partner in standard ready posture (kuda kuda).*

*Training partner delivers slow and controlled forehand slash to your high line.*

*Execute Basic Training Drill #3 Karambit Buah.*

*Bring attacking arm to optimum control position.*

# PART TWO

---

# COMBAT
# STRATEGY
# AND
# INTERMEDIATE
# SKILLS

---

## Changing Elevation

As previously mentioned one of the most important elements of training with the Karambit is the element of mobility. Not just moving the feet but also the changing of elevation.

Have you ever walked up behind someone and stood on their right side behind them, but tapped them on the left shoulder from behind and they looked in the direction of the tapping but you were standing on the exact opposite side? How about the doorbell rings and you open the door and there's nobody standing there and then you look down and to your surprise a little kid is standing there with his mom running up behind him on the walkway. These are excellent examples of the concept of changing elevation and mobility—the trickery of Pencak Silat. Such "trickery" or what Guru Besar Suwanda called "cheating," gives the Karambit practitioner a distinct advantage over his adversary.

There are two elements to change in elevation: Sell your adversary on where your position is. Then when he buys it End up not being where he expects to find you.

This gives you a tremendous tactical advantage as reaction is always slower than action. The second you've got him reacting, that is, looking for you, then you've turned the tables in your favor.

In order to accomplish this "sell and buy" task there are several drills available for training.

> *"He who takes action takes control of the fight*
> *as his adversary is busily reacting."*
> —Guru Besar Herman Suwanda

CHANGING ELEVATION DRILL #1
(FORWARD KNEELING)
This particular drill is used to develop forward positional advantage while changing elevation.

*Training partner (armed with LAMECO forearm guard and training knife) gauges for long range and then delivers a slow and controlled forehand slash to your highline.*

*Step forward to about your ten o'clock position at his OUTSIDE with your lead leg first. The drop to a solid Harimau three point kneeling position at the same time switching the Karambit to extended position (palm vertical) and catching his arm guard with the inside edge and tip of the Karambit.*

*Your head and upper body should be clearly out of the way of the delivery and your lead hand should be palm down applying pressure to the back of his forearm as your Karambit inside edge applies pressure upward in order to immobilize his weapon arm.*

## CHANGING ELEVATION DRILL #2 (BACKWARD KNEELING)

This particular drill is used to develop forward positional advantage while changing elevation.

*Face your partner in basic Kuda Kuda with Karambit in hand.*

*Training partner (armed with LAMECO forearm guard and training knife) gauges for long range and then delivers a slow and controlled thrust to your centerline.*

*Step backward to about your seven O'clock position at his OUTSIDE with your rear leg moving first. Then drop to a solid Harimau three point kneeling position at the same time switching the Karambit to extended position (palm vertical) and catching his arm guard with the inside edge and tip of the Karambit.*

*Your head and upper body should be clearly out of the way of the delivery and your lead hand should be palm down applying pressure to the back of his forearm as your Karambut inside edge applies pressure upward in order to immobilize his weapon arm.*

Key points to successful development of change in elevation skills:

Always assume a rock solid three point kneeling stance as discussed in earlier chapters. You don't want to be floundering around on the ground looking for some stability when you may need to switch gears again immediately and change direction in a split second.

Drop down and away from the attack. Down is good but dropping straight down may place you right smack in the middle of a flight path of an incoming strike. It's imperative that you move in such a manner as to position yourself both down and away from the attack in either direction.

Timing—the most important issue of these three—don't be in the same place at the same time a strike is on its way. This sounds rather pedantic and easier than it truly is. However, talk to a professional boxer or goal tender in professional sports about timing. It's all about being in the right place at the right time.

## *Tactical Operation*

When operating a Karambit during mobility it is essential to keep your Karambit at or about your line of sight. Similar to firearms defensive training tactics; when it comes time for either a tactical or speed reloading of a spent or inoperable magazine, all manipulation of the handgun is executed at or above eye level so as to keep the attention and visual field of the operator in the firefight even during reload.

The same concept applies to the manipulation of the Karambit. Even though it can move swiftly from one position to another and from retracted to extended and back again to retracted, it does you no good if you can't see where you're placing the edge or the tip.

You can flip and turn and pull off beautiful and fancy moves all day long, but if your not scoring placement on intended targets that you're behind the power curve and racing to get caught up. This is especially crucial in a self-defense setting where sight alignment and placement is essential to your personal well-being. Again, operate the Karambit within the field of your vision or within the line of your sight.

*Hold Karambit within your field of vision retracted and with support hand located directly behind Karambit*

*Regardless of manipulation it is imperative to keep the Karambit within your field of vision when in motion.*

## A Word About Timing

There are many good examples in our every day life of timing. Let's take for example pulling up to a railroad crossing just as the red lights start to blink and the bell rings. If you make it through before the train gets there—then good timing. If you don't make it through before the train gets there then bad timing—problem.

Another example would be driving up to a set of traffic lights changing color. Attempting to scream through a yellow light before it turns red requires timing. If you mis-time the switching of lights—especially if there's a cop sitting behind you, then not only do you have bad luck, but also bad timing or a problem.

Against the discretion of their parents, little kids play a timing game with their fingers and a slow moving fan blade. The object is to stick your finger in the fan between the blades and pull it out before the blade swings by again. If you have good timing then you win. If you mis-time the blades it can be rather uncomfortable at best.

Thus bad timing is synonymous with problem. The same applies for operation of the Karambit. If you find yourself in a self-defense situation, you need to be in the right place at the right time. If your timing is off—the consequences can be problematic at best.

Let's say someone's taking a swing at your head with a baseball bat. If your head is NOT occupying the same place at the same time as the incoming bat, then great timing—no problem. If your melon IS occupying the same space at the same time as the incoming bat, then bad timing—problem.

If a guy is swiping at your face with a knife, then you want to move out of the way BEFORE the knife gets there. Another method is to block or deflect the knife DURING the strike. But, if you wait until AFTER the swipe to get out of the way or block/ deflect, then it's too late—bad timing.

Thus, there are three positions of timing: BEFORE, DURING and AFTER. These can all be used to your advantage if you have a clear understanding—or used against you if you do not.

If you change elevation BEFORE he figures out where you are then good timing. If your body position and Karambit happen to both be set up in the right place DURING an event then good timing. If you pop out of nowhere and occupy "the space in his face" AFTER he swipes, punches or kicks—then good timing. There is literally a time and position in space BEFORE, a time and position in space DURING and a time and position in space AFTER an event. These are often referred to as the three points of "the triangle of timing" in the Filipino training method.

According to the teachings of the older Sundanese masters such as Pak Akyat and others, there is a mental aspect of training in Pencak Silat with regards to matter, energy, time and space whereby we can allegedly develop our innate abilities to manipulate the relationship between ourselves, matter, energy, space and the three points of time (BEFORE, DURING and AFTER) in a specialized study known as "Kebatinan." This study further teaches that there is a "BEFORE," an "AFTER" and a variable-length space in between the two (called "NOW") that can be adjusted by varying levels of perception.However that's enough information to fill another training manual.

For purposes of our physical training here with the Karambit, suffice it to say that a solid command of your physical position BEFORE, DURING and AFTER can give you the distinct advantage in any self-defense scenario.

## Mobility (Body Movement with the Karambit)

Knowing how to grip and operate the Karambit are essential building blocks but not the only elements of effective usage. Body movement with the Karambit is probably the most important in any engagement.

### MOBILITY DRILL #1 (STEP TIMING)

Ask your training partner to gear up with two LAMECO forearm guards and a training knife in each hand. Now, ask him to gauge for CLOSE range and deliver a slow and controlled thrust to your centerline.

*Facing your training partner one foot forward, Karambit forward in front of other hand and closer to your training partner and in the opposite hand of your lead foot.*

*Training partner lunges forward toward your center delivering a slow and controlled thrust to your centerline. Step to his outside, parry down and away and catch hook of Karambit in palm down hand position with your body to the outside.*

*Training partner again lunges forward toward your center this time with the opposite training knife in a slow and controlled manner. Again step to his outside, parry down and away and catch hook of Karambit in palm up hand position with your body to the outside.*

Repeat the above steps until you run out of space, switch positions with your partner and run the drill in the opposite direction.

More often than not you will be moving very quickly and in several different directions and/ or elevations when operating the Karambit. One of the unique features of the Karambit is that it can get you a couple inches closer to your target area with out you having to change your body position simply by switching from retracted to extended position.

This next drill helps develop mobility, placement and timing as well as transitioning from neutral retracted to extended operational posture at close range.

### MOBILITY DRILL #2 (STEP TIMING WITH RETRACTION AND EXTENSION)

Ask your training partner to gear up with two LAMECO forearm guards and a training knife in each hand. Now, ask him to gauge for CLOSE range and deliver a slow and controlled thrust to your centerline.

*Facing your training partner one foot forward, Karambit forward in front of other hand and closer to your training partner and in the opposite hand of your lead foot.*

*Training partner lunges forward toward your center delivering a slow and controlled thrust to your centerline. Step to his outside, parry down and away, switch from retracted to extended postion and catch hook of Karambit in palm down hand position with your body to the outside.*

Training partner again lunges forward toward your center this time with the opposite training knife in a slow and controlled manner. The second he moves transition the Karambit back into retracted position

*Again step to his outside, parry down and away switch to extended position and catch hook of Karambit in palm up hand position with your body to the outside.*

Training partner again lunges forward toward your center this time with the opposite training knife in a slow and controlled manner. The second he moves transition the Karambit back into retracted position.

*Repeat the above steps until you run out of space, switch positions with your partner and run the drill in the opposite direction.*

Key training points:

Always try to end up on the outside—safest place to be in a fight.

Maintain rigidity of arms (do not collapse your elbow) when making contact.

Training in Pencak Silat more often than not pays strict attention to the reality of multiple attackers. Although we'll get into this in much more detail later, it is important to develop an understanding of direction change at this point in your training.

## MOBILITY DRILL #3 KIRI-KANAN (DIRECTIONAL SIDE-TO-SIDE)

(Mande Muda Kuda Kuda Satu) Can be executed in either JURU or BUAH form.

Requiring two training partners geared up in LAMECO training gear and training knives.

Gauging from CLOSE range, one training partner delivers slow and controlled mid-line thrust with one hand and using the Karambit come to the inside while you move to the outside as in earlier drills.

*Begin in wide horse stance (Kuda Kuda Satu) with partners on either side of you at 90 degrees. Both gauge for close range.*

This particular drill is designed to familiarize the practitioner to the beginning stages of multiple attacks and to develop your peripheral vision at close range.

*One training partner delivers a slow and control thrust to your centerline. Using your peripheral vision, turn to the side that twitches first and quickly pivot on the flat of your feet to classic Kuda Kuda standing position facing in that direction. Position your hands such as that your body is on the outside and your training partner's weapon hand is on the inside down and away from your centerline. Remember to end up on the outside and in total control of the attacking arm.*

*Turn back to center—again in a wide horse stance (Kuda Kuda Satu) with partners on either side of you at 90 degrees.*

*Now the other training partner delivers a slow and control thrust to your centerline. Using your peripheral vision, turn to that side and quickly pivot on the flat of your feet to classic Kuda Kuda standing position facing in that direction. Position your hands such as that your body is on the outside and your training partner's weapon hand is on the inside down and away from your centerline. Remember to end up on the outside and in total control of the attacking arm.*

*Turn back to center—again in a wide horse stance (Kuda Kuda Satu) with partners on either side of you at ninety degrees.*

This drill is initially run in order where each training partner takes turns delivering one after the other in order. However, once this becomes second nature (gets really boring at high speeds), ask your training partners to alternate deliveries. Sometimes the guy on your left will deliver three times in a row and sometimes the guy on your right will deliver every other one and have them just keep switching patterns of delivery so as to make your job in picking up movement out of your peripheral vision more and more of a developed skill each time you train this drill.

It is highly suggested that you begin by asking your training partners to deliver one after the other in order when first training for multiple attackers. The next step is for them to alternate their timing so that you do not become motor-set. The most advanced level of this drill is to not know who is going to move and when they finally do, you have sensed this through your peripheral vision and you arrive exactly where you need to be at the exactly right timing. Once you have achieved this goal it's time to add forward and backward directional movement.

## MOBILITY DRILL #4 (DIRECTIONAL FORWARD AND BACKWARD)

(Mande Muda Kuda Kuda Dua) Can be executed in either JURU or BUAH form. Again requiring two training partners.

Gauging from CLOSE range, one training partner delivers slow and controlled mid-line thrust with one hand and using the Karambit come to the inside while you move to the outside as in earlier drills. This particular drill is designed to familiarize the practitioner with the reality of forward and backward motion in the event of multiple attackers at close range.

*Begin in standard position Kuda Kuda posture with one partner in front of you and one partner behind you.*

*Your forward-positioned training partner steps forward and delivers a slow and controlled centerline thrust. At the same time you step back and to his outside and position the Karambit and opposing hand as in previous exercises.*

*This same training partner again steps forward and delivers a slow and controlled centerline thrust. At the same time you step back and to his outside and position the Karambit and opposing hand as in previous exercises. Be sure to end up on the outside and in a superior controlling position at the end of your technique.*

Your backward-positioned training partner steps forward and delivers a slow
and controlled centerline thrust. Pivot on the flat of your feet and then step back and
to his outside while position the Karambit and opposing hand as in previous exercises.

That same training partner again
steps forward and delivers a slow
and controlled centerline thrust.
At the same time you step back
and to his outside and position
the Karambit and opposing hand
as in previous exercises.

Your forward-positioned training
partner (who has by now reposi-
tioned for further training) steps
forward and delivers a slow and
controlled centerline thrust. Pivot
on the flat of your feet and then
step back and to his outside
while position the Karambit
and opposing hand as in previous
exercises. Continue this flow
of movement back and forth
between both partners.

As in the previous drill, it is suggested that you first drill each side in order, one partner before the other with each one taking an additional step and then switching to the other side. As you become more proficient with this drill ask you partners to alternate their timing and change deliveries at random. This advance stage of mobility and directional training is designed to develop forward and backward mobility and awareness of multiple attacks.

## MOBILITY DRILL #5 (HARIMAU KNEELING)
### (Harimau One) JURU ONLY
This is one of the best training JURUs available to develop your Harimau kneeling technique with the Karambit. This is the first in a series of twelve Harimau Jurus as taught by Guru Besar Herman Suwanda to those wishing to progress to other more complex systems.

*Start from classic Harimau position with Karambit retracted. Be sure to establish solid three point stance.*

*Drop lead knee down and come to Anak Harimau posture.*

*Raise opposite knee and transition
Karambit to forward position.*

*Drop lead knee down and come
to Anak Harimau posture.*

*Pivot on knees to opposite direction.
Remember to keep Karambit in
front of all other body parts.*

*Drop lead knee down and come
to Anak Harimau posture.*

*Pivot on knees again to the previous position.*

*Step knee back to starting position with Karambit retracted.*

## Beginning Takedowns

Once an understanding of grips, operation, mobility and direction is achieved, the next level of training is to begin your study of takedowns.

Terminology such as styles or types of movements are generally indicative of a village names or famous Silat teachers' names from West Java. As an example Cikalong is the name of a village who's practitioners of Pencak Silat tend to execute techniques entering (MASUK) from the outside position. Another example would be Cimande—named after a village in West Java noted for its superior and well-respected use of the forearms and strong legs derived from villagers practicing their system while standing in a flowing nearby river. Additionally is the example of Sha Bandar (sometimes spelled Syabandar)—the name of a prominent Pencak Silat Practitioner who preferred to enter from the inside position to execute technique. There are others such as Madi (jumping or "flying" style developed by a superior Pencak Silat instructor allegedly of diminutive stature), Kari ("Scissors hands" style) and Serak to name a few.

Thus in our study of takedowns, you will notice the names of that particular style are employed to describe the technique associated with that style.

### SERIES I—CIKALONG (OUTSIDE ENTRY USING NO DISARMING)

**Elbow Displacement—make sure your elbow blocks any upward movement.**

*Face your training partner and gauge for close range.*

*Training partner (wearing LAMECO training gear) while holding a training knife proceeds to deliver a slow and controlled thrust toward your centerline.*

*Step to his outside and execute Basic Training Drill #2.*

*Now step forward (down and away) into a perfect three-pointharimau kneeling stance while simultaneously (carefully and with good control) placing the tip and/ or inside edge of the Karambit in the crook of your training partners arm and sandwiching the back of his weapon arm triceps just above the elbow as you pull him downward.*

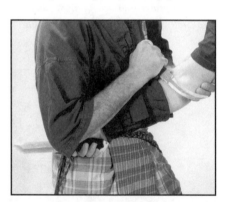

*Be sure of your placement of Karambit and support hand to control his elbow and use your forearm to prevent his knife from moving upward.*

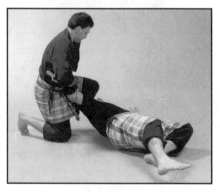 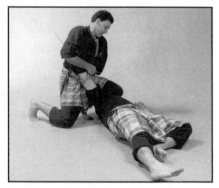

*Now that he's down you may need to further control his body by switching your knee over his head to prevent him from sitting up.*

## Hip displacement

*Face your training partner and gauge for close range.*

*Training partner (wearing LAMECO training gear) while holding a training knife proceeds to deliver a slow and controlled thrust toward your centerline.*

*Step to his outside and execute Basic Training Drill #2.*

*Now step forward (down and away) and prepare for a perfect three-point harimau kneeling stance while simultaneously (carefully and with good control) placing the tip and/ or inside edge of the Karambit at the exact point of your training partners nearest hip bone while sandwiching the back of his weapon arm tricep just above the elbow as you pull him downward via pushing forward with the Karambit.*

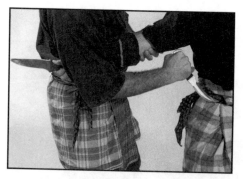

*Be sure of your placement of Karambit and support hand to control his elbow and use your forearm to prevent his knife from moving upward with the tip secured into the hip bone area. Be careful not collapse your weapon arm on the way down.*

*Again execute the takedown using the Harimau three point stance using your weight pushing against the hip bone to displace his weight backwards.*

*Now that he's down you may need to further control his body by switching your knee over his head to prevent him from sitting up.*

### Tuhod—Knee displacement (karambit extended)

*Face your training partner and gauge for close range.*

*Training partner (wearing LAMECO training gear) while holding a training knife proceeds to deliver a slow and controlled thrust toward your centerline.*

*Step to his outside and execute Basic Training Drill #2.*

*Extend and lower the Karambit toward the inside position of your partners knee. Remember to be mindful of controlling his weapon arm throughout this technique.*

*Now step forward (down and away) in preparation for a perfect three-point harimau kneeling stance while simultaneously (carefully and with good control) placing the tip and/ or inside edge of the Karambit at the exact point of your training partners nearest knee (on the inside) and sandwiching the back of his weapon arm tricep just above the elbow as you pull him downward via pushing his knee outward with the Karambit.*

*Be sure of your placement of Karambit and support hand to control his elbow and use your armpit (lat muscles) to prevent his knife from moving upward while simultaneously placing the extended tip securely into his inside knee area. Be careful not collapse your weapon arm on the way down into Harimau as this will help soften his fall.*

*Now that he's down you may need to further control his body by switching your knee over his head to prevent him from sitting up.*

## *Disarming with the Karambit*

During one of our training sessions together, one of the greatest edged weapons masters of our modern times Punong Guro Sulite—said to me: "Steve, the thumb is the father of the four fingers. So when you control the father you can control the whole family." Although a Filipino training principle, this exact same technology is true of the Indonesian system of knife disarming called Sabatan.

Our ultimate goal in disarming with the Karambit is two-fold in purpose:

- *Don't get cut*
- *Remove the fang from the snake (as they say in the training circles)*

One of the most important aspects of disarming with the Karambit is to do all of your technique and manipulations DOWN AND AWAY from your own body. Pushing the knife away simply invites him to swing right back in the other direction. Pushing the knife down simply invites him to come up another path. However, executing a disarm both DOWN and AWAY from your body gives you the much desirable advantage of maximum amount of space between you and that sharp edge or point coming at you.

The very first step is to always get your body out to a safe position, then reach for control of his weapon arm and finally "go hunting for the thumb" (as Pak Herman used to say) in order to control the "father of the four fingers." The Karambit is actually the very final step applicable only after these first three are accomplished.

Simple 4-step formula for disarming with the karambit:

1. *Get to superior position*
2. *Control the weapon arm*
3. *Secure four fingers base of the thumb*
4. *Apply opposing pressures with the Karambit and your grip on his thumb to strip his weapon out from his grip.*

Remember that disarming in itself is an art form. Guru Besar Suwanda often brought the class through the basics of first understanding the basic movements of controlling the weapon arm (Sabatan system) long before he focused us on "hunting for the thumb."

According to Guru Besar, it was just as important if not more important to merge into the flow of an incoming strike and assume control prior to any further application of technique. Even when studying disarms we are reminded again of the training progression—"we must walk before we can run..."

## SERIES II—SYABANDAR (INSIDE ENTRY WITH DISARMING)

**Elbow displacement with disarm—make sure your elbow blocks any upward movement.**

*Face your training partner and gauge for close range*

*Training partner (wearing LAMECO training gear) while holding a training knife proceeds to deliver a slow and controlled forehand slash to your high line.*

*Step to his outside and execute Basic Training Drill #3.*

(a.) Slide the Karambit down his weapon arm to the edge of the training knife controlling his arm all the way

(b.) while simultaneously taking four fingers grip on his weapon thumb and

(c.) pull with that hand back toward you and

(d.) push forward with the Karambit edge stripping the training knife out of his grip.

Now that the knife has been disarmed step forward (down and away) into a perfect three-point harimau kneeling stance while simultaneously (carefully and with good control) placing the tip and/ or inside edge of the Karambit in the crook of your training partners arm and sandwiching the back of his weapon arm triceps just above the elbow as you pull him downward.

Be sure of your placement of Karambit and support hand to control his elbow and use your forearm to prevent his weapon arm from coming into play.

Now that he's down you may need to further control his body by switching your knee over his head to prevent him from sitting up.

## Hip displacement with disarm.

*Face your training partner and gauge for close range.*

*Training partner (wearing LAMECO training gear) while holding a training knife proceeds to deliver a slow and controlled forehand slash to your high line.*

*Step to his outside and execute Basic Training Drill #3.*

*Slide the Karambit down to the edge of the training knife controlling his arm.*

Pull with your four-fingers-grasping hand as you push forward with the Karambit stripping the training knife out of his grip.

Now that the knife has been disarmed step forward (down and away) into a perfect three-point harimau kneeling stance while simultaneously (carefully and with good control) placing the tip and/ or inside edge of the Karambit against your training partners nearest hip bone and sandwiching the back of his weapon arm triceps just above the elbow as you pull him downward.

Be sure of your placement of Karambit and support hand to control his elbow and use your forearm to prevent his arm from coming into play.

Now that he's down you may need to further control his body by switching your knee over his head to prevent him from sitting up.

### Tuhod—Knee displacement (karambit extended) with disarm.

*Face your training partner and gauge for close range.*

*Training partner (wearing LAMECO training gear) while holding a training knife proceeds to deliver a slow and controlled forehand slash to your high line.*

*Step to his outside and execute Basic Training Drill #3.*

*Slide the Karambit down to the edge of the training knife controlling his arm.*

*Then assume four fingers grip on his weapon thumb and pull with that hand as you push forward with the Karambit stripping the training knife out of his grip.*

*Now that the knife has been disarmed step forward (down and away) into a perfect three-pointharimau kneeling stance while simultaneously (carefully and with good control) placing the tip and/ or inside edge of the Karambit against the inside of training partners nearest knee and sandwiching the back of his weapon arm triceps just above the elbow as you pull him downward by pulling outward on his knee with the Karambit.*

*Be sure of your placement of Karambit and support hand to control his elbow and use your armpit (lat muscles)to prevent his arm from coming into play.*

*Now that he's down you may need to further control his body by switching your knee over his head to prevent him from sitting up.*

## *Intermediate Takedowns*

### SERIES III—CIKALONG (WITH DISARMING)
  1. Strip then "what if he punches"
     a. Outside to standing straight arm bar

*Face your training partner and gauge for close range.*

*Training partner (wearing LAMECO training gear) while holding a training knife proceeds to deliver a slow and controlled forehand slash to your high line.*

*Step to his outside and execute Basic Training Drill #3.*

*Slide the Karambit down to the edge of the training knife controlling his arm.*

(a.) Then assume four fingers grip on his weapon thumb
and pull with that hand as you

(b) push forward with the Karambit stripping
the training knife out of his grip.

(c) Here, your training partner, upon realizing that his knife
has been stripped away starts to swing at you with his other fist.
Raise your lead hand to the outside of his incoming punch.

Step to his outside, pivot your body and
grab his wrist with your lead hand as you
use the Karambit to immobilize his arms.

You should be facing in the same direction
as he is and pushing slightly forward
to keep him off balance and down and
away from you using the inside edge
of the Karambit to take him down
using standing straight arm bar.

### SERIES III-1.B FIRST OPTION—OUTSIDE FOOT PLACEMENT

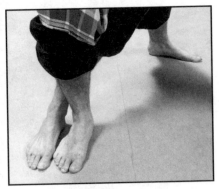

*Same technique as in Series III—1.a. You should end up facing in the same direction as he is and pushing slightly forward to keep him off balance and down and away from you using the inside edge of the Karambit.*

*Now step behind his supporting leg with your near leg and push with the standing arm bar to take him down.*

### SERIES III-1.C. SECOND OPTION—OUTSIDE FOOT PLACEMENT PLUS EXTENDED KARAMBIT HOOK TO BACK OF KNEE

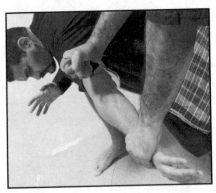

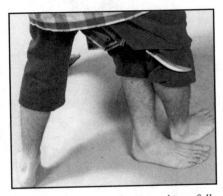

*Same technique as in Series III—1.b. You should end up facing in the same direction as he is and pushing slightly forward to keep him off balance and down and away from you using the inside edge of the Karambit.*

*This time transition the Karambit to full extension placing the inside edge against the back of your training partners knee and then step behind his supporting leg with your near leg and push with the standing arm bar to take him down.*

### Series IV—Harimau Tangan (with disarming)
1. Strip to double arm lock in front

*Face your training partner and gauge for close range.*

*Training partner (wearing LAMECO training gear) while holding a training knife proceeds to deliver a slow and controlled forehand slash to your high line.*

*Step to his outside and execute Basic Training Drill #3.*

*Slide the Karambit down to the edge of the training knife controlling his arm.*

Then assume four fingers grip on his weapon thumb and pull with that hand as you push forward with the Karambit stripping the training knife out of his grip.

Here, your training partner, upon realizing that his knife has been stripped away starts to swing at you with his other fist. Raise your lead hand to the outside of his incoming punch.

Stay in the same position you are at his outside and pick up the incoming punch with your Karambit.

Push his incoming hand (with your Karambit) under your support arm and lock it to his other arm with your elbow.

*Now replace your elbow with the inside edge of the Karambit and push forward while simultaneously pulling back with your grabbing hand.*

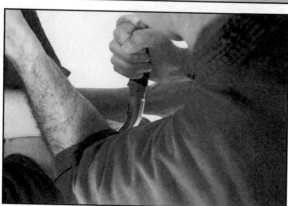

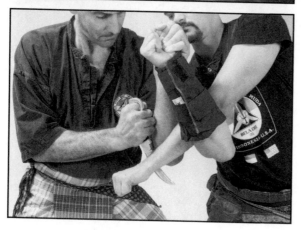

# Part Three

## Advanced Application

Before we jump into this final section of training with the Karambit, there are a couple of training issues I'd like to bring to your attention.

First is a reminder about training partners. Sometimes it can be difficult to even find a training partner, so when you do have someone to work with, endeavor to treat their bodies with respect. Remember, that it will soon be his turn to try the technique on you as a training partner. Should you not have a partner to train with—no problem—that's where your jurus come in. You can even practice with your training Karambit while watching TV—spinning it back and forth from retracted to extended position and back again.

When working these techniques with a partner always go slow and controlled—especially the very first run through because neither of you know what to expect. Go easy on the shoulders and knees as these are the first joints to give up as the years of hard training on your body adds up. We only get one body per lifetime. It's up to you and the partners you work with to train smart and train safe.

Second is a just point of interest for those planning on training in Indonesia regarding an extreme dissimilarity in training practices between Westerners and the native peoples of West Java. One of the most curious things I noticed during my training trips in Indonesia was how nobody ever tapped out from pain. They would sort of yelp or say "ouch" instead. Later on I found out that in their culture tapping the ground during training loosely translates to "ok really put it on—I can take more" and if you don't tap means that you've had enough. It's the exact opposite in the West whereas if you're ready to submit you tap the mat. Just remember where you are when you reach down to tap out!

## *Escapes with the Karambit*

Similar to any other self-defense aid such as a pepper spray, pocket knife, firearm, etc., it is the responsibility of those who carry the karambit for self-defense to be as highly trained and proficient as possible in its usage.

The most practical application for any such defensive implement is if you are assaulted. There are many ways to handle an assault situation, however, the best is to evade. If you cannot evade or you were taken by surprise or simply overpowered, then your next best option is to escape.

This next section presents some of the more common street scenarios and techniques for using the Karambit to aid in your escape.

## KARAMBIT ESCAPE # 1

*Attacker grabs your wrist with his mirror hand and is about to strike or pull at you.*

*Turn your grabbed arm hand palm up and deploy your Karambit.*

*Pull your grabbed hand up and back toward you at the same time you place the inside edge of the Karambit under your opponents wrist using the inside edge and push upward.*

*Keep pulling your hand away as you push out and away with the Karambit using the hook to free yourself from his grasp.*

## Karambit Escape # 2a

*Attacker grabs with both hands around your throat. Secure his outside hand by grabbing his wrist with one hand and deploy your Karambit with the other hand.*

*Lean your shoulder into his center as you slam the Karambit upward into groin positioning inside edge and/or tip directly on target.*

## KARAMBIT ESCAPE # 2B

Attacker grabs with both hands around your throat. Secure his outside hand by grabbing his wrist with one hand and deploy your Karambit with the other hand.

Switch position to extended Karambit and begin to lean forward as if pushing a car uphull with both hands.

Lean your shoulder into his center as you slam the Karambit upward into his throat positioning inside edge and/or tip directly on target.

### KARAMBIT ESCAPE # 3

*Attacker grabs both your shoulders and begins to draw you closer to his body.*

*Deploy your Karambit and from retracted Karambit position deliver a hammer fist strike to the groin area.*

*When his head comes forward from the groin strike, reach up and grab the back of his head and push down as you dislodge the Karambit from his groin.*

*Push down on the back of his neck and vertical palm strike with the Karambit upward placing inside edge/ tip against attacker's throat to either negotiate or continue through should you feel your life be in immediate danger.*

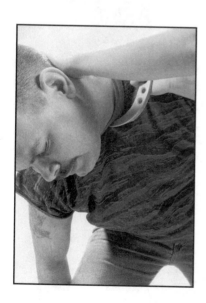

*You can also push down on the back of his head with your other hand as the Karambit is moving upward against his throat and just leave it there should you need the added security of controlling your opponent prior to your escape.*

## KARAMBIT ESCAPE # 4A.

*Attacker grabs you, puts you in a headlock while pushing you downward and starts dragging you to a van with an open door and the engine running.*

*Deploy your Karambit as you push forward with your nearest knee directly into the back of his near knee—don't be afraid to kneel using all of your weight into the back of his leg.*

*Simultaneously transition to extended Karambit pulling the inside edge/hook up into his groin. The opposing pressure of your knee going forward and your extended Karambit driving up directly into his groin will most likely cause some type of reaction allowing you the opportunity to flee.*

## KARAMBIT ESCAPE # 4B.

*Attacker grabs you, puts you in a headlock while
pulling you upward and starts
dragging you to a van with an open
door and the engine running.*

*If you are of diminutive stature in comparison
to your attacker and you cannot reach or he
is too large to buckle his knees from behind,
then reach up over his far shoulder with your
extended Karambit and hook his throat (or
his eyeball—if you feel your life is in danger)
palm down with the edge or tip inserted
and pull vigorously until he lets you go.*

## KARAMBIT ESCAPE # 5

*Attacker gets you in a double arm bear hug from behind pinning both your arms and lifting you off ground.*

*Deploy your Karambit and start digging under the webs between his fingers.*

*Bury the Karambit deeply into his hand violently twisting and peel his hands apart with the tip.*

## KARAMBIT ESCAPE # 6

*Attacker gets you in double arm bear hug from behind under both arms, but not lifting you off the ground. Immediately deploy Karambit.*

*Maintain retracted grip and slam the Karambit into the back of his hand. If he still doesn't release you, then bury the tip deeply between his fingers under the web and start ripping it around while continually pushing the tip and sharp edge deeper into his hands and forearm.*

*He lets go but continues to try and grab you again.*

*Hammer fist your Karambit into his groin and then run away.*

*He grabs your leg to prevent you from running so you place your free hand behind his neck pushing his head further down as you pull your Karambit up from his groin and directly into his throat.*

## Kuncis (locks)

Pronounced (Koon-Chee) a Kunci literally translates to "lock" or "lock and key." There are two general categories of kuncis—those executed on the high line above the waist (arm, shoulder, elbow, neck, etc.,) and those executed on the low line (Knees, hips, ankles, etc.,) below the waistline. Kuncis may be applied to any joint in the body on any arm or any leg, toes or fingers. Their purpose is to tie up your opponent so that he is immobilized. Sometimes they submit as a result of discomfort (due to pain) or sometimes as a result of mechanical influence.

One of the most popular sayings in Indonesian Pencak Silat is that "the upper body influences the lower body and the lower body influences the upper body." What this means is that if you get somebody tied up on the highline say with an arm lock, then that's going to influence where his legs go when he tries to move. On the other hand if you lock up one of his legs and he is immobilized but still moving in a forward direction (as an example) then his upper body will continue its forward momentum.

## NOMENCLATURE OF TECHNIQUE

Many times when training with the Indonesian masters, I would ask "Sir, what do you call this one" or "what is the name of this technique?" Occasionally the answer was something you could jot down in your notebook and ask him the proper spelling. However, the majority of the time the answer was usually something like "you do like this…" and then they would again demonstrate the technique. At the risk of being disrespectful I would dare not ask a second time.

So that leaves you with the problem of "What do I call this one?" and sometimes you try and find something that either fits or that maybe someone else you studied with has a name for it that would work. For example, in this following section entitled "Highline Defense," all of these Kunci's were given to me with no names in Indonesia, but luckily having seen somewhat similar movements as a long term Maphilindo Silat student under Guro Dan Inosanto at the Inosanto Academy of Martial Arts in Los Angeles, California, I took the liberty of naming them what Guro Inosanto calls them or their very close relatives.

Let's take the term "Chicken Wing" as an example. It is my understanding that the original term was passed down to Guro Dan Inosanto by Judo Gene LaBelle many years ago as Guro Inosanto indicated in one of his Maphilindo Silat classes (Tuesday/ Thursday nights at his training academy in Los Angeles). As a side note for those curious about this type of Silat, "Maphilindo" is an acronym created by Guro Dan Inosanto representing the blend of MA-laysian, PHIL-ippine, and INDO-nesian arts of Silat he studied over the last three decades.

"Chicken Wing" fits a similar empty-hand technique here and it works in this particular application so I adopted it only for purposes of nomenclature in separating it from other techniques. However, as a matter of respect, I think it's a good idea to always give credit where credit is due to the originator and/ or lineage from which a technique or terminology was derived.

## High Line Defense
### SERIES I—ARM LOCKS (WITH DISARMING)
**Strip to chicken wing**

*Face your training partner and gauge for close range.*

*Training partner, while holding a training knife, proceeds to deliver a slow and controlled backhand slash to your high line. Step to his outside and execute Basic Training Drill #1.*

*Slide the Karambit down to the edge of the training knife controlling his arm and assume four fingers grip on the base of his thumb.*

*Then with four fingers grip on his weapon thumb, pull with that hand as you push forward with the Karambit stripping the training knife out of his grasp.*

Maintain your four fingers grasp and wrap your thumb around his thumb maintaining a "pistol grip" as you push his palm down and away from your body toward behind his own back.

Using the inside edge of your Karambit against the crook of his bent arm, push straight upward thus raising his arm and creating a space.

Now that the knife has been disarmed and you are controlling his arm with your raised Karambit, let go of your "pistol grip" on his thumb and step forward thrusting your left hand under your opponent's raised arm into the space you just created.

Continue pushing your left arm all the way through and then force his shoulder down as you pivot your body to the extreme outside and behind your training partner now facing the same direction as he.

Place the Karambit on or about the side of his head while maintaining the Kunci with your left arm.

## Strip to turkey wing

*Face your training partner
and gauge for close range.*

*Training partner, while holding
a training knife, proceeds to deliver
a slow and controlled backhand slash
to your high line. Step to his outside
and execute Basic Training Drill #1.*

*Slide the Karambit down to the edge
of the training knife controlling his
arm and assume four fingers grip
on the base of his thumb.*

*Then with four fingers grip on his weapon
thumb, pull with that hand as you push
forward with the Karambit stripping
the training knife out of his grasp.*

*Maintain your four fingers grasp and wrap your thumb around his thumb maintaining a "pistol grip" as you push his palm down and away from your body toward behind his own back as you thrust your Karambit arm through toward his back.*

*Push up with your Karambit arm and continue stepping behind.*

*Lock up his weapon arm by pulling up with the Karambit and insert your other hand over his free shoulder pulling him in toward you.*

*Move closer to his body ending up directly behind with your Karambit arm locking his weapon arm and your other hand securing his head by turning his chin away so that he cannot move toward you.*

## Strip to double arm lock behind

*Execute same exact technique and disarm as in previous technique. From this position, again punch your Karambit under his right arm and begin moving your body around to his back at the same time.*

*Continue to move around his body and reach behind him grasping his opposite elbow from behind.*

*Transition the Karambit to extended position thrusting your Karambit arm completely under your training partner's weapon arm and hook his support arm with your Karambit in the palm down hand posture while maintaining grip of his triceps with your other hand.*

## SERIES II—BUAH TANGAN SUPULUH (WITH DISARMING)
### Jurus Tangan Sepuluh (#10)—Arm Break

*Face your training partner and gauge for close range.*

*Training partner (wearing LAMECO training gear) while holding a training knife proceeds to deliver a slow and controlled centerline to your high line.*

*Step to his outside and execute Basic Training Drill #2.*

*Slide the Karambit down to the edge of the training knife controlling his arm.*

*Then assume four fingers grip on his weapon thumb and place your Karambit on the edge of his knife (or the digits holding his knife).*

*Pull with your four-fingers-grip hand as you push forward with the Karambit stripping the training knife out of his grip.*

*Now that the knife has been stripped, push his hand palm down and away from your body maintaining control of your training partners hand.*

*Place the Karambit inside edge (vertical palm) up above your training partner's elbow and pull his arm by the triceps (using your Karambit) into your body as you release your left hand.*

*Turn your left hand palm up and raise
it toward your face continuing to pull
in his arm using your Karambit to pull
his extended arm into the crook
of your left elbow.*

*Once in position, grasp your right
shoulder with your left hand. Raise
your entire body up and locate your
Karambit elbow directly over his exposed
elbow (which should by now
be pointing directly upward).*

*Drop both your body and right elbow
down as if to sit in a chair while pushing
up with your left arm effectively applying
pressure to your training partner's
extended weapon arm.*

### Jurus Tangan Supuluh (#10)—Hip Hook

*Execute the same exact technique as above. Once in position, with the Karambit in retracted position, grasp your right shoulder with your left hand and drop your weight.*

*Extend the Karambit and push your Karambit elbow past his elbow as you reach forward and down.*

*Place your Karambit tip onto your training partner's nearest hip bone and push forward until he begins to feel off balance.*

## Jurus Tangan Supuluh (#10)—knee hook (extended Karambit)

*Execute the same exact technique as above.*

*Once in position, with the Karambit back into retracted position, grasp your right shoulder with your left hand and switch the Karambit to the extended position.*

*Lean further forward and point the tip down.*

*Hook the inside of his knee and gently pull toward your body until he feels slightly off balance.*

## Low Line Defense
### SERIES III—HARIMAU PROGRESSION (WITH DISARMING)
### 1. Technique: Strip to Ledok Harimau

*Training partner while holding
a training knife proceeds to deliver
a slow and controlled slash or
thrust to your high line.*

*Execute Sysbandar Masuk (inside entry).*

*Step to his outside and execute
Basic Training Drill #2.*

*Slide the Karambit down to the edge
of the training knife controlling his arm.*

*Then assume four fingers grip on his weapon thumb and pull with that hand as you push forward with the Karambit stripping the training knife out of his grip.*

*Now that the knife has been disarmed transition to DUDUK (seated Harimau) wrapping the lead leg with your leg and insert your other leg to trip him backward.*

*Place your Karambit palm down with inside edge pressing against inside of training partner's knee.*

*Push outward with the Karambit and lean your body outward until he starts to feel off balance.*

### Technique: Strip to Tuhod Harimau

*Execute exact same technique
as above up until the leg wrap.*

*Now place the bottom of your left foot
on the side of the near foot of your
training partner and flip the Karambit
to the extended position.*

*Place your Karambit inside edge/ tip
on the inside of his knee as you drop into
DUDUK posture (seated position).*

*Apply slight pressure against the knee
until he begins to feel off balanced.
Remember to keep your arm straight
during the takedown.*

**Technique: Tuhod Harimau failure backup**

*Execute exact same technique except let's say that you missed the extended Karambit hook to the knee and blew right past his knee with your Karambit altogether.*

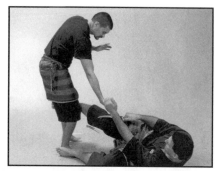

*Continue your motion down and away turning onto your hip.*

*Place the laces of your right foot against the inside of your partner's near leg in the exact same position where the Karambit would have been had you not missed it or it slipped off.*

*Continue turning your body applying slight pressure with the top of your foot on the inside of his knee until he becomes off balance.*

*Follow-up with Karambit covering his centerline ready to intercept any possible counter strike.*

**Technique: Strip to attempted Tuhod Harimau counter response.**

*Execute exact same technique where you extended Karambit hook to the knee in an attempted takedown.*

*He sees what's going on end steps forward with his other leg to avoid the inevitable.*

*Extend your far leg outside. Extend the Karambit and place the Karambit palm up on the inside and behind his leg.*

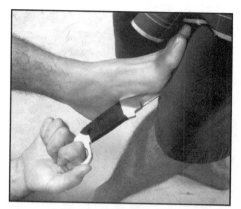

*Step on spine of Karambit with near foot.*

*Your other leg is blocking his forward momentum and your body weight is driving the Karambit.*

*Apply pressure with inside edge of your Karambit against the back of your partner's lead leg using your foot to push until he loses balance.*

## Advanced Options

### SERIES IV—CIKALONG PROGRESSION (WITH DISARMING)

Cikalong "C"-clamp takedown.

*Face your training partner and gauge for close range*

*Training partner, holding a training knife, proceeds to deliver a slow and controlled thrust toward your centerline.*

*Step to his outside and execute Basic Training Drill #2.*

*Disarm knife.*

*Continue through disarming controlling four fingers base of his thumb to a pistol grip.*

*Using the Karambit and your other hand pass his extended arm under your near leg.*

*Grasp his hand with your palm up so that his palm is drawn upward and pull up tightly against your leg as you lock the back of your knee down on top of his forearm.*

*Place the Karambit palm down on his clavicle which should help him fall back slowly to the deck (allow him time to break his fall—remember this is your training partner— not an actual opponent).*

*Step toward the ground with your raised leg.*

*Keep pulling up on his arm tight to your leg and pivot your body into his neck placing your other shin against his neck.*

## Cikalong "C"-clamp takedown to knee spread.

*Execute the same exact technique as above.*

*Now continue by bringing your shin closer into his neck until you feel tension. Maintain upward pressure on his arm against the inside of your leg. The Indonesian term for this type of "wrapping pressure technique is "LILIT" and can be applied to any limb.*

*Finally, point your knees in opposite directions and sit down as if you're going to sit in a chair. This simple movement applies tremendous pressure on your training partner so be aware when he's had enough.*

### Cikalong "C"-clamp takedown to pancake flip.

*Execute the same exact technique as above.*

*While maintaining upward pull on his arm against the inside of your leg step over his head with your other leg.*

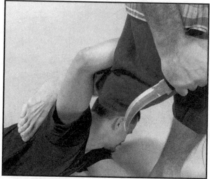

*As soon as your foot is on the ground lift your other leg so as to brush the laces of your foot against his armpit which will begin to rotate his body.*

*Continue your rotation until he ends up face down (prone) and come to Harimau kneeling. This applies a tremendous amount of pressure on his shoulder so be very careful. Use your hands on the ground for support if you feel off balance executing this part of the technique.*

**Cikalong "C" clamp takedown to negotiation posture.**

*Execute the same exact technique as above.*

*Now reach back with your free arm and grab the back of his other arm and lift up.*

*Insert your other leg under that arm and now let go with your hand.*

*Continue turning your
body counter-clockwise
to seated posture.*

*Sit straight down while tightly constricting
both your legs thus binding both his arms
preventing any strikes or escape.*

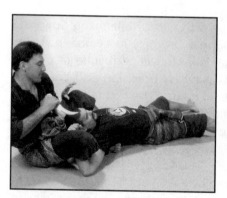

*Insert your free hand palm up under
his neck and push upward thus
preventing and opportunity for
him to kick or roll out of it.*

*This is what I call a
"negotiation posture."*

## Closing Concepts

In closing, the secret to higher-level skills is in the number of repetitions. Modern psychologists estimate that the human body must execute a determined movement approximately one thousand times before it starts to sink in. These movements can be anything from tying your shoes, to swinging a baseball bat, playing the guitar or even a Pencak Silat Karambit technique.

These same scientists claim that the second thousand repetitions is when something begins to grove into the mind as almost second nature. By the third thousandth repetition, they say it's pretty much an unconscious act and that it has burned itself deep enough into the psychological and physiological structure of the body that it becomes a natural fluid movement not requiring any thought or attention from the mind. Some refer to this as "unconscious competence."

However, like all motor skills, such as swimming, running, playing billiards, etc., these are all perishable skills. Even after you hit the three thousandth repetition mark and you don't train for a couple of years, your timing, skill, placement, and fluidity can fade—it all goes away.

After dinner one night, training with Guru Herlanbang Suwanda (Guru Besar Herman Suwanda's younger brother) in Lembang, I was watching him execute a phenomenal Pak Monyet technique of biblical magnitude at incredible speed with flawless precision and control. I humbly asked him if he would please do it again. He nodded, smiled and pulled it off even faster and more fluid than the first time. Turning to the translator in total awe I asked her to please ask him how he developed such incredible speed and fluidity. "His reply," she said was "beyond countless repetitions."

It was much later explained to me by Pak Herman that training techniques are like small trickles of water in the dry sand. The more volume (repetitions) the larger the trickles become and begin to etch a small grove into the sand. With even more volume (more repetitions) the water begins to flow faster and the grove is worked even deeper into the sand.

In time, after many repetitions, that small stream of water turns into a rushing river that cannot be turned away.

To further continue your studies in the Karambit, Steve Tarani is currently available for private and group instruction. He can be reached at his office in California at 949-515-0905 or click on www.karambit.com for additional information.

# The Suwanda Academy

I n the midst of flying bullets, swinging blades and battle cries, a young
Indonesian warrior winces from a bead of sweat trickling down into
the cut above his right eye. Stealthily as a cat he climbs a rope hand-
over-hand to the deck of a Dutch warship careful not to give away his
position and his intentions. Cursing the pain and plunging himself deep
into a fiercely raging battle, a bullet grazes his left leg as he buries his
blade deep into the belly of his adversary.

Such was one of many typical hand-to-hand combat experiences for
Uyuh Suwanda, Indonesian Freedom Fighter and founder of Mande
Muda Pencak Silat—the Suwanda family system.

During the fight for independence, Guru Besar Pendekar Uyuh
Suwanda (my master's father) and other Indonesian freedom fighters like
him in the 1940's, literally battled tooth and nail for the independence of

*Guru Besar Suwanda
with Jagabaya Steve
Tarani at his training
academy, in Irvine,
California in 1995.*

*Guru Besar Herman Suwanda in classic Mande Muda
Pencak Silat fight postures.*

their country. The personal combat system of these remarkable warriors was the indigenous and efficient fighting system of Indonesian Pencak Silat.

In particular, the Suwanda family system, codified by Pendekar Suwanda, can be traced back to what is known as *Ma'en Po*. Originating from the indigenous Sundanese ethnic group circa mid 14th century, the backbone of this unique fighting system was born in the heartland of West Java. Over the ensuing centuries, neighboring villages independently developed their own systems and styles such as *Cikalong, Kari, Madi, Serak* and *Syahbandar* (from Sumatra).

Each system has its own specialty. *Cipecut*, for example, emphasizes usage of flexible weapons, whereas *Rikesan* focuses primarily on locks and pressure points. Still other systems emphasize close quarter combative elements like striking such as *Tanjakan* and on the more mental or spiritual aspect *Timbangan* and *Ulin Napas* (spiritual breathing/ meditation).

Long before the end of the Dutch occupation, Pendekar Uyuh Suwanda had realized the importance of cross-training in the various Pencak Silat villagesystems. Very similar to the modern concept of *Jeet Kune Do* as brought forth by Bruce Lee in the 1960's and 70's and Sifu Dan Inosanto in the 1980's through today, the idea of "using no way as way" and "take what is useful" was a way of life for Pendekar Uyuh Suwanda.

At the end of the war, he continued to study with various Pencak Silat Master instructors in research and development of the Suwandasystem to the extent of combining key combative elements of 18 individual systems to form the Suwanda family system which is known today as Pencak Silat Mande Muda.

Literally translated as "a growing and evolving art with its beginning roots in Cimande," the idea behind Mande Muda Pencak Silat (the Suwanda family system) is that any fighting system worth it's salt, must continue to change both from within the system and from outside the system. In other words, the same boxing techniques used by John L. Sullivan at the turn of the century are not applicable to the world boxing champions of today. Fighting styles change and any effective system will develop to adapt to these changes. Much like the rifle of Daniel Boone, although a superior weapon for its time, is no match for the modern M4 Carbine, so is it the case for the ancient fighting arts which must adapt to any newly developed combat technologies. Pendekar Uyuh Suwanda recognized the importance of this evolution and thus designed the Mande Muda system to be able to call upon the battle-readiness of 18 individual systems and easily morph the skills of the fighter into whatever was necessary to get the job done.

In the early 1960's, my master a then-young Herman Suwanda, the eldest son of Pendekar Uyuh, was the first recipient of this multi-system training. He was trained not only by his father, who continued to travel to different villages in search of effective systems, but also by other masters who were invited by his father to come to his village and teach. It became quite taxing to continually travel to each village and try to train students at the same time in all the different disciplines. The solution was simple, to create one school where all the masters could come to teach in one location. Back then, it was a revolutionary concept and the dream of the founder of Pencak Silat Mande Muda International.

Unfortunately, Guru Besar Pendekar Uyuh Suwanda, passed away before he could begin the monumental effort that it would take create such an academy of training. However, the idea planted a seed in the mind of the heir to the Mande Muda system—Guru Besar Pendekar Herman Suwanda. Having begun his training in Pencak Silat at age five, throughout the sixties and seventies, Herman Suwanda observed the teaching methods of the ancients—backyards, rice paddies, tea fields and if ever in a large location it was usually in the gymnasium of a college or university (which was quite diluted as any curriculum had to conform to university policy). The true art of Pencak Silat, the core substance, was taught in living rooms. One cannot open a Yellow Pages and find a Pencak Silat school in Indonesia. It is traditionally a family art, passed down from grandfather to father to son/ daughter.

Asked by his father to travel from village to village and gather the knowledge of the masters over the decades, Herman Suwanda never forgot the dream of his father. He too recognized the tremendous advantage of having it all in one place—the masters, the traditional training—all without any compromise of integrity as a result of government or university policies. It was a noble dream for both father and son and a necessity for the continued freedom of self, family, village, and a sovereign nation.

In the nineteen seventies, many attempts were made by Pendekar Uyuh Suwanda to set the wheels in motion. Acquiring the property and the financial backing to establish such a facility proved to be an enormous task. Imagine the continual uphill battle in trying to ask the government or some massive industrial corporation for a grant or loan to develop property for such non-profit and esoteric usage. The dream appeared unattainable, the ideal was too high and even if it was the best way to preserve the old teachings, it wouldn't generate any substantial revenue, so why would any government or private enterprise invest in such an unprofitable endeavor?

Years later, after the passing of his father, Guru Besar Pendekar Herman Suwanda, while continuing to expand Mandu Muda from 18 to 24 sub-systems, single-handedly disseminated the Mande Muda system throughout the United States and Canada. After many years of teaching seminars to countless interested Americans, Mande Muda is now considered one of the most widely practiced Pencak Silat system in North America.

Mande Muda Pencak Silat emphasizes the physical fighting techniques (Buah), Jurus (forms) and Kembangan (combination forms) or Ibing (Sundanese for Kembangan). However, the most important element of the Mande Muda system is nothing you can put your fist through. It is as elusive as the wind and as difficult to train as a wild tiger—this is the character of the student. Only about 3/4 of the Mande Muda system offers the student training in the physical arts of striking, locking, throwing, grappling, jumping and weapons. The remaining 1/4 of Mande Muda are the chisel and hammer (meditative breathing drills) given to the student in which to carve the raw granite of self into a disciplined practitioner. The ultimate goal of Mande Muda Pencak Silat is to create enough mental and spiritual discipline in a student to develop noble character and understanding of self. It is an important principle of Mande Muda that skill is not as important as being of noble character.

The question remains the same now in 2001AD as it did in 1943— How is it possible to bring a student weather indigenous or foreign, to understand the deepest and highest teachings of the masters, steeped in the Indonesian culture without compromising the integrity of the art? The answer remains the same—establish a school in a central location to the villages where the student can experience total immersion and hands-on training with the few remaining masters of Pencak Silat.

The problems also remain the same. Pencak Silat is the product of poor villagers out in the country. There are barely roofs over the heads of the masters who preserve the ancient ways. Compounded by a capricious political climate, Indonesia is wrought with economic injustices which, as in every shift of political power in history, takes its toll on the poor. Basic amenities such as food and shelter are denied to even the most needy.

In previous years the Indonesian economic collapse thrust thousands of families into starvation as the value of the Rupiah plummeted to an all-time low. Relying on the typical Indonesian mentality of trying to make the best out of what little is available, Pendekar Suwanda turned a tragedy into an advantage by purchasing Indonesian property with American dollars (which where very strong in value during the collapse) and hiring architects to design plans. The foundation was established. The dream of two generations was about to become a reality.

Work was begun immediately on the digging and setting of the foundation for the Suwanda Academy. However, as fate would have it, not too long after initial stages of construction, the Indonesian Rupiah regained value and thus multiplied the cost of the construction project through the roof.

Pendekar Suwanda was faced with several problems. The cost of the project had risen considerably beyond any projected budget. More and more families in the village were without food and clothing as the value of the Rupia dropped and inflation took its toll on the most desolate.

What most seminar participants throughout the 1990's in the west never realized is that Pendekar Herman Suwanda personally supported his entire immediate family and an extended 60 families in the village community who can barely afford a handful of rice a day. Mande Muda membership and training fees ended up directly in the mouths of the poorest villagers.

The Indonesian government does not fund public education. Much like the way the American government refuses to support socialized medicine, the Indonesian government refuses to support the elementary education of its sons and daughters. While driving through the streets of Jakarta it is commonplace for travelers to be solicited by street vendors ranging from ages 4 and up. When I first saw this I asked "Why aren't these little kids in school?" The hard cold fact is that kids need to hit the streets in order to first pay for food for the family—education is a secondary consideration.

The first and most difficult problem to resolve was how to continue supporting the poorest families of the village—basic food, shelter, clothing and education. Next was how to continue funding the Suwanda Academy construction project which would eventually provide jobs and educational opportunities for the villagers. Lastly, the ancient art of Pencak Silat was beginning to die off along with the old masters who had no place to pass on the art except to a select few in their primitive "living rooms." So many problems and way too much responsibility for a single Master.

Pendekar Suwanda responded by working harder and smarter. He maximized his seminar schedule to as much as he could physically handle so as to transfer as much as he could to compensate for the rise in provisional costs. He organized food and clothing drives and set up collections for donations in the United States and Canada to be sent directly to Indonesia's poorest.

Choosing between 15 and 17 of the most destitute families, Pendekar Suwanda consulted with the village leaders to determined which families were the most destitute. These were the first to receive a box of rice. As the food and clothing project progressed, Pendekar took pictures of the families being clothed and fed and brought these back to the U.S. to show that the donations and contributions were in fact reaching their destination. Soon more groups were formed and more Americans became interested in supporting the project. The difference of only $200 to $300 American dollars can feed as many as 100 families. The one particular village for which Pendekar Suwanda is responsible is comprised of approximately 5,000 families—donations are still needed to this very day.

The second problem was basic education. If someone gave you the responsibility of using your martial art skills to provide basic education to a hundred kids, how would you do it?

Pendekar Suwanda had a solution: once the Suwanda Academy was built, it was his plan to personally "hire" students to attend the academy to learn their own heritage, Pencak Silat. The sponsorship monies would then be given directly to the dean of the schools (in order to bypass any middle-man dipping into the coffers) for that particular kid to ensure a basic education of reading and writing. This kills two birds with one stone: the kid gets a much needed degree of basic literacy and gains the knowledge of his Indonesian heritage in becoming an instructor of Pencak Silat. Administratively, donations are divided in percentages to feed the poor, provide basic education and preserve the art of the ancients. Skillfully orchestrated in such a manner as to avoid the sticky fingers of an unstable political atmosphere, a detailed selection process is carried out so as to truly reach those who are in need. It is one of the rare incidences of our modern times that a martial arts organization channels its resources toward such humanitarian application.

The third problem solved by the Suwanda Academy, is the preservation of true Indonesian Pencak Silat. The academy is open to any indigenous and authentic Indonesian Pencak Silat Master who wishes to share his art with students who are interested. Foreigner and local villager alike benefit from the rare opportunity to train hands-on with the old masters.

On March 21,2000 my master Guru Besar Pendekar Herman Suwanda and his wife Shannon passed away as the result of an automobile accident in Germany. The ongoing construction of the Suwanda academy, the dream of his father and one of the most important goals of his life is now completed.

The Suwanda Academy, is comprised of 9 bedrooms, 5 bathrooms, a kitchen facility and a massive training hall where the masters conduct classes five days a week according to the old traditions. This provides an excellent opportunity especially for foreigners who are interested in total immersion training in Pencak Silat in West Java.

Long before even the plans for the academy were drawn up, we used to train in Guru Besar's back yard in Lembang. Now, fortunately, those who wish to study the ancient arts of Indonesian Pencak Silat are provided with an excellent and rare opportunity to train hands-on at this impressive and pristine training facility.

There are two branches of instruction available in the Mande Muda family system today. One is Mande Muda Pencak Silat International, by which Pendekar Herman Suwanda's family members are available for scheduled seminars at your school or dojo. The other is direct training in Indonesia under the few remaining masters in person at the Suwanda Academy located about 90 miles southeast of Bandung, West Java in the small village of Cibodas (this name literally translates to "white waters").

It is a rare and unique opportunity to train at the Suwanda Academy. As an Indonesian-trained instructor directly under the tutelage of Gur Besar Suwanda it is my honor and privilege to lead students (who are truly seeking) to the source. Those interested may contact me directly at stevetarani@earthlink.net or click on www.karambit.com or www.suwandaacademy.com for more information.

# ABOUT THE AUTHOR

*Jagabaya Steve Tarani*

A student of edged weapons since 1979 Steve Tarani trained exten-
sively throughout the 1980s in the Filipino weapons arts under the
likes of Guro Ted Lucaylucay and Grandmaster Giron resulting in his
achievement of graduate/ instructor status in 1989 under Grandmaster
Leovigildo Miguel Giron. Further research, training and investigation into
various Japanese, Chinese, Burmese and other edged weapons systems
led him to the masters of the Karambit hailing from the Indonesian
Archipelago. About this same time, Steve began "formal" training in the
Malaysian and Indonesian systems with his first Malaysian instructor Cigku
Sulaiman Sharif.

While a dedicated Maphilindo Silat (and Filipino Escrima) student
training directly under Guru Dan Inosanto in Los Angeles, California,
Steve was introduced to Guru Besar Herman Suwanda by Guro Inosanto
and became a devoted disciple. Jagabaya Tarani trained with his new
teacher throughout the 1990's up to and until the passing of his master in

March of 2000. Although trained predominantly in the US, Steve was often encouraged by personal invitation, to train with Guru Besar Suwanda, his family and his teachers in Indonesia.

Captivated by the traditional training methods and total immersion into the Indonesian culture, Steve trained in Indonesia directly under the likes of Pencak Silat Masters such as: Pak Akyat, Pak Odid, Bapak Suherman and others and became intimately familiar with the styles and techniques of the ancients. Receiving his instructorship in Lembang, Jawa Barat, Indonesia in July of 1996, he continued in his studies to achieve the rank of Jagabaya—innermost guard of the Pendekar.

An international educator, specializing in edged weapons systems from around the globe, Steve Tarani is a full-time law enforcement trainer and Defensive Tactics consultant. His many students are as fascinated as he was by the mysterious Karambit and repeatedly ask him to share in his knowledge about it. Traveling and teaching all over the world, Steve never had the opportunity, until he was invited by CFW Enterprises Inc., to produce the very first instructional video series and training manuscript on the Karambit—exotic weapon of the Indonesian Archipelago.

Steve Tarani is available for seminars and can be reached at stevetarani@earthlink.net or by clicking on www.karambit.com.

*Author's photos.*

*Pak Mahmud.*          *Pak Mahmud and*          *Bapak Suherman*
                       *Pendekar Suwanda*         *Lembang, Indonesia*
                       *in Cimande village.*